AN

HISTORICAL AND CRITICAL

ACCOUNT

OF

A GRAND SERIES

OF

NATIONAL MEDALS.

Published under the Direction of

JAMES MUDIE, ESQ.

AND DEDICATED BY PERMISSION

TO HIS MOST EXCELLENT MAJESTY

George the Fourth.

———

EMBELLISHED WITH

OUTLINES OF THE ENTIRE SERIES.

———

LONDON:

PUBLISHED BY HENRY COLBURN, AND CO., CONDUIT STREET.

———

1820.

TO HIS MOST EXCELLENT MAJESTY
GEORGE THE FOURTH.

SIRE,

Under your Majesty's auspicious Government the British arms achieved a succession of Victories over the most powerful enemy with whom this country ever contended. These Victories terminated in his surrender and downfall. A series, of Medals, important in design and execution, transmitting the record of such momentous and glorious successes to Posterity, wanted only the gracious sanction of your Majesty's encouragement and protection, to give them their due value in the estimation of the British People. This honor, conferred upon the only private individual who has ventured upon so important and national an undertaking, your Majesty has graciously and spontaneously been pleased to afford.

Duly sensible of this gracious condescension, I beg leave to offer to your Majesty the grateful homage of

Your Majesty's

Dutiful and devoted Subject,

JAMES MUDIE.

London, August 15, 1820.

List of Subscribers to the Medals.

HER LATE MAJESTY THE QUEEN.
HER ROYAL HIGHNESS THE PRINCESS OF HESSE HOMBURG.

Her Grace the Duchess of WELLINGTON.
The Most Noble the Marchioness of EXETER.
The Right Honourable the Countess de GREY.
Lady SOPHIA PIERREPONT.
Lady TAYLOR.
Lady WARBURTON.
The Honourable Mrs. KENYON.
The Honourable Mrs. ROBINSON.
The Honourable Miss ANNE RUSHOUT, Northwick.
Mrs. BROWN, Paris.
Miss BROWN.
Mrs. Gen. CROSBIE, Bristol.
Miss RICHARDSON CURRER.
Mrs. DODSWORTH.
Mrs. GREEN, Leicester.
Mrs. K——.
Miss LAWRENCE, Studley Park.
Miss ROBINSON.
Miss SCOTT, Rose Lodge, Cobham.
Miss SELBY.
Miss WETTENHALL, Chester.
Mrs. WOOD, Potter Hill, near Perth, North Britain.

HIS MAJESTY GEORGE THE FOURTH.
HIS ROYAL HIGHNESS THE DUKE OF YORK.
HIS ROYAL HIGHNESS THE DUKE OF SUSSEX.

His late Royal Highness le Duc de BERRY.
His Grace the Duke of BEDFORD.
His Grace the Duke of WELLINGTON.

b

The Most Noble the Marquis of ANGLESEY.
The Most Noble the Marquis of EXETER.
The Most Noble the Marquis of HUNTLEY.
The Right Honourable Earl BATHURST.
The Right Honourable Earl BEAUCHAMP.
The Right Honourable Earl MANVERS.
The Right Honourable the Earl of RADNOR.
The Right Honourable the Earl of ROSEBERRY.
The Right Honourable the Earl of VERULAM.
The Right Honourable Earl ST. VINCENT, K. G. C. B.
The Right Honourable Viscount CLIVE.
The Right Honourable Viscount HARBERTON.
The Right Honourable Lord APSLEY.
Marshal General Lord BERESFORD.
The Right Honourable Lord COMBERMERE.
Admiral Lord EXMOUTH.
Lieutenant General Lord HILL, G. C. B.
The Right Honourable Lord MARK KERR.
Lieutenant General Lord LYNEDOCK, G. C. B.
The Right Honourable Lord MACDONALD.
The Right Honourable Lord JAMES MURRAY.
The Right Honourable Lord Viscount PALMERSTON.
The Right Honourable Lord PORCHESTER.
Le Baron DENON, late Director of the Louvre.
The Right Honourable NICHOLAS VANSITTART.
Sir A. ALLAN, Baronet, M. P.
Sir J. ASTLEY, Baronet.
Sir W. CHATTERTON, Baronet, County of Cork.
Sir THOMAS SLINGSLY, Baronet.
Sir J. TWYSDEN, Baronet, Sittingbourne.
Sir C. ROBINSON, M. P.
Lieutenant General Sir GEORGE BECKWITH, G. C. B.
Lieutenant General Sir GEORGE MURRAY, G. C. B.
Lieutenant Colonel Sir U. BURGH, K. C. B.
Major General Sir H. TORRENS, K. C. B.
Vice Admiral Sir SIDNEY SMITH.
The Honourable Mr. PETRE.

Allan, John, Esq. United States.
Ames, Levi, jun. Esq. Clifton.
Atherley, George, Esq. Southampton.
Atkinson, J. Esq. Cookham.
Bamforth, Mr. Leeds.
Bankes, M. Esq. Wigan.
Barber and Whitwell, Messrs. York, 12 sets.
Barclay, C. Esq. Clapham.
Barratt and Son, Messrs. Bath, 4 sets.
Barrow, Captain J. Manchester.
Bateman, J. Esq. Manchester.
Baugh, B. Esq. Bristol.
Beever, T. B. Esq. Hethel Hall.
——, Esq. Liverpool.
Bevan, Dr. M. D. Monmouth.
Bewes, T. Esq. Beaumont Lodge, near Plymouth, 2 sets.
Bindley, the late James, Esq. F. S. A.
Blades, John, Esq.
Blick, Rev. F. Tamworth.
Bolongaro, Mr. Manchester, 11 sets.
Booth, Mr. Duke-street, 2 sets silver.
Booth, B. Esq. Manchester.
Bradfute, J. Esq. Edinburgh.
Brockett, T. Esq. Newcastle.
Brooke, Rev. Dr. Horton, near Bristol.
Brookes, T. L. Esq. Mere Hall, Cheshire.
Brown, D. Esq. Newcastle.
Bunn, J. Esq. Frome.
Burney, Rev. C. P. Greenwich.
Burton, R. Esq. Sacket Hill House, Margate.
Campbell, Lieut. Gen. Duncan, 3 sets.
Campbell, A. Esq. 2 sets.
Carmalt, Rev. W. Putney.
Cave, J. Esq. Brentol.

Chinney, G. R. Esq.
Clark, J. Esq. Manchester.
Clarke, Rev. Mr.
Claxton, B. Esq. Henbury.
Clayton, W. Esq.
Compton, H. Esq. Manor House, Hampshire.
C——, Rev. W. Cambridge.
Friend of ditto, ditto.
Cririe, W. Esq. Manchester.
Cunliffe, Foster, Esq. Langollen.
Currer, Rev. D. R.
Cussans, T. Esq.
Daniel, T. jun. Esq. Bristol.
Darby, F. Esq. Colebrooke Dale.
Davies, Mr. John, Bath.
Dent, J. Esq. M. P. 2 sets, silver and bronze.
Disney, J. Esq. Hyde, Essex.
Eaton, Mr. Worcester.
Empson, A. Esq.
Farquhar, T. Harvey, Esq.
Ferrers, Rev. E. Chariton, Hants.
Finlay, K. Esq. M. P.
Fisher, G. jun. Esq. Clifton.
Folkard, W. Esq. Suffolk.
Forbes, C. Esq. M. P. 2 sets, silver and bronze.
Forster, Mr. W.
Freeling, Francis, Esq.
Garry, N. Esq. Conduit-street.
Gordon, Mr. A.
Gordon, John, Esq. Wincombe.
Gray, E. Esq.
Greaves, T. Esq. Manchester.
Grosett, J. R. Esq. Laycock Abbey.
Gutch, J. M. Esq. Brislington.
Hammont, H. Esq. Norwich.

Hankinson, Rev. R. A. M. West Bilney Lodge, near Lynn, Norfolk.
Harding, J. Esq. Manchester.
Hardman, T. Esq. Manchester.
Harrison, Rev. H. B. Northampton.
Hay, Rev. W. R. Ackworth.
Hawkins, E. Esq. Nutfield, Surrey.
Heatley, W. Esq. Manchester.
Henderson, J. Esq.
Hervey, late Col. 14th Dragoons.
Hill, J. jun. Esq. Bristol.
Hope, Thomas, Esq.
Hope, Henry P. Esq.
Hughes, E. H. B. Esq.
Hurst, Thomas, Esq.
Hurt, Charles, jun. Esq. Wirksworth.
Hunt, T. W. Esq. Oxford.
Hunt, R. Esq. Stoke Newington.
Irvine, H. Esq. Dublin.
James, Major, Gloucester-place.
Johnson, W. Esq.
Jolmes, J. Esq. Retford.
Jones and Forrester, Messrs. Hull.
Jones and Sons, Messrs. Liverpool, 7 sets.
Kortright, the late ——, Esq.
Lamb, Rev. D. Northamptonshire.
Larken, E. Esq. Tottenham Green.
Lee, General.
Lechmere, E. H. Esq.
Leeke, ——, Esq.
Lettsom, S. F. Esq.
Lewis, J. E. Esq. Bristol.
Long, Jones, Esq. Farley Castle.
Longdon, T. H. Esq. Shooters Hill.
Lubbock, Sir I. B. Bart.
Lyell, Charles, Esq.
Lyman, Thomas, Esq. United States.

Mc Dougall, H. Esq. LL. D. Dublin.
March, Thomas, Esq.
Marsh and Co. Messrs. Bankers.
Marshall, W. Esq. Tadcaster.
Massey, Mr. 2 sets, silver and bronze.
Metcalf, T. Esq. Delhi, India.
Miles, the late Mr. Richard.
Mills, John, Esq.
Mills, Mr. George.
Mitchel and Russel, Messrs. Glasgow, 4 sets.
M——, H. Esq.
Moore, D. Esq. Lincoln's-inn-square.
Morgan, Lieut. Col. Abergavenny.
Morton, Mr. Edinburgh, 4 sets.
Mozley, L. Esq. Liverpool.
Munday and Slater, Messrs. Oxford, 2 sets.
Murray, M. Esq. Leeds.
Nash, Edward, Esq.
Nichols, Mr. Wakefield, 3 sets.
Norris, T. Esq. Bury, Lancashire.
Norton, Mr. Bristol, 14 sets.
Page, Capt. R. N. Ipswich.
Paine, Mr. New York.
Parker, T. Esq. Cuerdon Hall.
Parton, James, Esq.
Paton, J. Esq. Montrose, North Britain.
Perry, James, Esq.
Phare, George, Esq.
Pitcher, J. G. Esq. 2 sets, silver and bronze.
Pooley, H. Esq. Manchester.
Popham, F. Esq. Clarendon Park.
Porcher, J. D. Esq.
Powell, J. P. Esq. Margate.
Powell, T. Esq. Manchester.

Pownall, Henry, Esq.
Raper, J. Lamplugh, Esq.
Ratcliffe, T. W. Esq. Manchester.
Reeve, Robert, Esq.
Reid, Mr. C. K. Newcastle, 6 sets.
Roberts, Mr. John, Bray.
Rouw, Peter, Esq.
Row, James, Esq.
Sainthill, R. Esq.
Salmon, W. Esq. Devizes.
Salvin, B. J. Esq. Durham.
Sams, Mr. J. Darlington.
Scargill, Lieut. 9th foot.
Sheppard, Rev. J. L. Cambridge.
Sibthorp, Colonel, M. P.
Slatter, T. Esq. Manchester.
Smallbone, Mr. 2 sets.
Smith, Rev. J. Newcastle.
Smith, R. Esq. Greenwich.
Solomon and Lewis, Messrs. 50 sets.
Solomon, Mr. Myer, 2 sets.
Sotheby, S. Esq.
Standen, James, Esq.
Standish, C. Esq.
Stewart, J. Esq.
Stokes, C. Esq.
Street, G. T. Esq.
Sullivan, L. Esq.
Taylor, G. W. Esq. M. P.

Taylor, J. R. Esq.
Taylor, John, Esq.
Thesiger, Aug. Esq.
Thomas, Colonel.
Thomason and Jones, Messrs. Birmingham, 2 sets.
Turner, T. Esq. Gloucester.
Uthoff, ——, Esq.
Wadmore, J. Esq.
Walker, J. Esq. M. P.
Watt, James, Esq.
Webb, Mr. Thomas, near Lichfield.
Wedderburn, Webster, Esq.
West, Mr. Dublin, 9 sets.
Whiteaves, Mr. Fleet-street, 93 sets.
Whitwell, Mr. York.
Wild, J. Esq. Clapham.
Willett, H. R. Esq. Lincoln's-inn-square.
Williams, Mr. G. 2 sets.
Williams, Marshall, Esq.
Willink, D. Esq. Liverpool.
Wilson, T. Esq. Newcastle.
Winn, C. Esq. Nostell Park.
Wyon, Mr. W. Royal Mint.
Yerbury, J. Esq. Shirehampton.
Young, Mr. M. 55 sets.
Zanetti and Agnew, Messrs. Manchester, 6 sets.

Those Ladies and Gentlemen who deferred subscribing until the whole Series was completed, are informed that they are now ready for delivery in Gold, Silver, or Bronze, at Mr. WHITEAVES', 30, Fleet Street; Mr. YOUNG's, 46, High Holborn; Messrs. SOLOMON and Co. 2, New Street, Covent Garden; at the Repository of Arts, 129, Pall Mall; Messrs. GRIFFIN and Co. 142, Leadenhall Street; Messrs. BARBER and WHITWELL, York; Messrs. REID and SON, Newcastle; Messrs. BRODIE and DOWDING, Salisbury; Mr. MORTON, Edinburgh; Messrs. BARRATT and SON, Bath; Messrs. JONES and FORRESTER, Hull; Mr. BAMFORTH, Leeds; Messrs. MUNDAY and SLATER, Oxford; Mr. NICHOLS, Wakefield; Messrs. JONES and SONS, Liverpool; Mr. EATON, Worcester; Mr. MATTHEW WEST, Dublin; Messrs. MITCHELL and RUSSELL, Glasgow; Messrs. NORTON and SON, Bristol; Messrs. ZANETTI and AGNEW, and Mr. BOLONGARO, Manchester; and Mr. L. CONGDON, Dock, Plymouth.

Medals in Bronze, 10s. 6d. each, or Twenty Guineas the Series, including an elegant case, arranged for the library or cabinet.

In Silver, one Guinea each, or Forty Guineas the Series.

In Gold, Fifteen Guineas each, or Six Hundred Guineas the Series.

*** SINGLE MEDALS MAY BE PURCHASED.

CONTENTS.

Introduction.

MEDALS would be well worthy of attention, were it only that they have been admired by many of the wisest and best men of ancient and modern times, by Pliny, Alfred, Petrarch, Camden, Selden, &c. But they do not require the approbation of the illustrious to recommend them to the admiration of the thinking and the tasteful. They have beauties innately and intrinsically their own, which, founded on the immutable principles of Nature, must ever afford delight to the human mind. Novelty, beauty, and sublimity are the three great sources of pleasure, and these are well supplied by Medals. It is the thirst of novelty that makes the mind so curious and eager in its researches into antiquity, and hence arises a great part of the pleasure which is derived from ancient Medals, displaying, as they do, the visages and forms of persons with whose minds history has made us so acquainted that we long to see the shapes and aspects of the bodies they inhabited, and of the faces on which their minds and characters were impressed. From a similar feeling we are delighted with their exhibiting the battles, honours, dresses, edifices, deities, religious rites, and innumerable other interesting circumstances belonging to them. The beauty, and sometimes the sublimity, of these objects give additional zest to the pleasure afforded by Medals—a pleasure which is the more relished in proportion as the mind and imagination are refined and vigorous. Hence the noblest people and states in ancient times, those of Greece and Rome, have been most distinguished for their attachment to, and production of Coins and Medals, a vast number of these having been spared by the destroyer

c

Time, to attest the pains and success with which they were executed, while
the circumstances they designated shew the importance they attached to
them.   From the same causes (though operating less strongly with regard
to the pleasure of novelty, fed as that pleasure is by an ardent desire to
look back into remote times) modern Medals afford a high gratification.
They, as well as ancient Medals, have not only excited the desire
of possessing them in such distinguished individuals as are above-men-
tioned, and in the directors of public libraries, academies, museums,
&c. but have recommended them to the regard of public rulers, who,
taking the Mint under their immediate superintendance and controul,
have used it as a means of heightening the splendour of their admi-
nistrations, of extending and perpetuating their civil and military
renown, and the real or assumed glory of their chief magistrate or
monarch. This was formerly the practice of the states of Italy, where an
ardent admiration of Medals arose, as was naturally to be expected, at the
time of the revival of literature and the fine arts, and to which the enthusiasm of Petrarch much contributed, who did not omit to include Medals
in his search after those works of the imagination and of philosophy which
were buried in Italian, Greek, and Asiatic cloisters, in the obscure possession of Greek artizans, and in the bosom of the earth. Of the present
governments of Europe, Russia and Sweden shew a just estimation of a
public mint, and the latter is promoting a subscription for the engraving of
a series of Medals in honour of great men in every country, and to which
the King has contributed five thousand pounds. Russia has issued Medals
in honour of National Victories of half the amount of the National Series
described in this work, and to which the Emperor has subscribed three
thousand pounds. But the French have been distinguished above every other
modern nation for a love of the numismatic art. Louis the Fourteenth employed the Mint to give medallic dignity to his successes in arts and arms,
and even to bronze over his disgraces, and record them on lying metal,

as if they were genuine honours. But their most distinguished medallic publication is the celebrated Napoleon Series of one hundred and sixty Medals, of the civil and military actions of that extraordinary personage, published chiefly from the designs and under the direction of Denon, director of the medallic mint under Napoleon, most of them beautiful in invention and execution. Indeed, so eminently distinguished are the French for their love of the medallic and the other branches of the arts, that M. Denon was elevated to the rank of a nobleman as a reward for his taste and talent in the fine arts. But the French do not rest satisfied with what is done—though so well done—by the government. Their taste and feelings must be gratified in the engraving and stamping of Medals relating to their own private occurrences, to objects of domestic history, endearment, and honour, to the success of well-laid plans of honourable profit and social felicity, to the happiness of nuptial alliances, and of the births of children. Indeed, the medallic, as well as the other branches of the elegant family of the Arts, join company with the happy household deities of the cheerful and tasteful French. In England no conception is formed how subservient Medals may be made to the honourable gratifications of private taste and feeling. Thus, as a particular instance, the portrait of a head of a family or of a friend may be struck, with this advantage above that of a print, that it is not easily damaged. It would resist even fire when the print would be destroyed by much less destructive materials. But England—the rival of France in intellectual energy and renown, who has trodden with at least equal success every other path of fame—England, it is to be regretted, has hitherto left this one almost unopened. Her SIMON in CROMWELL's time, it must be confessed, made a successful commencement in it, and much excellence crowned the endeavours of CROKER in the reign of ANNE; but since that time our Coinage and Medals have been little else but base in every thing except the Metal. Not that a people so eminently successful in every other Art and Science, and who in the sister Arts of Painting, Statuary, and Engraving, boast of their HAYDON, TURNER, WILKIE, CHANTREY, FLAXMAN, SHARPE, HEATH, LANDSEER, BROMLEY, COOKE, &c. can possibly want ability adequate to the highest Medallic attainments, if it be properly called forth and exercised. Messrs. WEBB, WYON, MILLS, and FAULKNER, have given sufficient evidences of the truth of this opinion, and there are some corroborative specimens in the Series of subjects of which the following pages are a description. Such are the busts of his Majesty and of Lord Lynedoch by Mr. Webb, the stormings of St. Sebastian and Badajoz, reverses by Mr. Mills, and the reverses to Lords Howe and Duncan by Mr. Wyon. But still the Publisher of this National Series was compelled to employ Foreign Artists chiefly, and some of the Heads, and the greater part of the Reverses were supplied by the talent of France, in order to avoid an extreme tediousness in bringing it out, and to give it every possible perfection, so as to render the work as beautiful as the same number of Medals of which it consists, taken at random from the Napoleon Series. It is therefore in point of execution, equally deserving of patronage with that Series, and more so of the English collector, as it has a mixture of British Medal engraving, and is in its subject, in the important circumstances it commemorates, altogether British, and worthy of the connoisseur to possess, whatever may be his political sentiments. For, besides the consideration that the beauty of a work of Art gives it a high value altogether independent of the subject, if the subject be no violation of morality or propriety, every one will allow that in the defeating of so formidable a power as that which NAPOLEON arrayed against Spain and England during the late war, there must have been a concurrent exercise of great talent and fortitude, and the possession of a noble work of art that honours such distinguished merit, is worthy of the moralist, the man of taste, and the Englishman. But notwithstanding the powerful recommendation which the National Series has to the patronage of the refined part of the British community, and the country at large, the Proprietor has had a very inadequate remuneration for his great trouble and expence in bringing out so large a work, most of his engravers of which resided in France, and were of a high class of excellence. The relish for the Fine Arts in England has progressively increased during the last fifty years, as is evident from the establishment and gradual increase of the numbers and improvement of our Artists and Exhibitions, but still the public attachment to Art is very limited, and most so to the Medallic branch of it. Were it not so, the Proprietor would not be now urging this complaint after the completion of a Series of Medals that would have been worthy of the government itself to have brought out. He would not have had it in his power to state that even among those whom it might have been reasonably expected would have been the readiest to promote it, the individuals who have been recorded in the Series, only a very small number have honoured it with their support *. A very icy feeling indeed must be prevalent, when to the high recommendations of the beauty and novelty of such a work, one of the strongest motives that influence, upon all other occasions, the human breast, is altogether dormant; that of praise, and praise too such as the most exalted among mankind have been proud of obtaining. Medals are the least perishable of all the materials upon which the artist displays his powers, and makes the visible depositary of his genius. They continue current on

---

* But he must be permitted to state here, that had it not been for the friendly and tasteful liberality of a distinguished Banking-house, and of an independent Member of the House of Commons well known for the extension of his bounty, not only at home, but even to the shores of India, the Proprietor must have stopped short in the progress of this National work.

There are indeed very few who have any idea of the extremely slow progress of Medal engraving. Many of the artists employed in this series have been several months in finishing one reverse, and for which they have received more than £.100, and the proprietor, in addition to six years devotion of his time and trouble, has expended upwards of £.10,000.

the tide of time when every production of every other art has sunk into oblivion. When Apelles, in speaking of the exalted excellence at which he aimed, said, " I paint for eternity," he could only have referred to that prolongation of fame which is obtained by the highest efforts of genius, and not to the evanescent productions of his pencil. But had the materials he used been as lasting as that which is adopted by the Medallist, his allusion might not have been altogether inapplicable to them, even admitting it to have been uttered, as the words were, in the enthusiasm of his art. First rate, then, as the series is in subject, in execution, and in durability, the Proprietor submits them, together with the following description, to the consideration and public spirit of his countrymen in general, and to the regard of the tasteful part of them in particular. Excepting a set of Medals commemorative of the Duke of Marlborough's victories, and struck by the command of Queen Anne, they are the only series upon a given subject in honour of England, ever published by an English subject, and they are the only one that ranks high as a work of art. To suffer it therefore to be received merely with the lukewarmness of its present limited encouragement, would be to check, if not to destroy, any further endeavour to advance the taste for this beautiful branch of the Fine Arts in our country; or, at least, to prevent any similar honour being conferred upon the distinguished among its inhabitants. It would be to cut off one of the elegant and valuable sources of reward to merit, and to stop up one of its most beautiful and lengthened channels of fame. It would be, in fine, a contradiction to the very spirit of enterprise, and of dignity, which the National Series commemorates, and to that character for reflection which the people of England have ever sustained. The thoughts of such an anomaly we will no longer—we cannot, maintain. That fine taste which is so extensively and feelingly exercised by the well educated among our countrymen in the encouragement and enjoyment of every other species of Art and Literature, cannot, from its close alliance with Medals, but be exercised upon them also. For that purpose it is only requisite to have attention properly invited to them, and this is the object of the following work. Private and Public Feeling, Classical Reading and Recollection, the beauties of Art, every thing that is rational and dignified, recommend this charming art to their esteem. Who can resist such motives ?

HISTORICAL AND CRITICAL ACCOUNT

OF

MR. MUDIE'S NATIONAL MEDALS.

Pl. 1.

I

II

III

IV

Normand fils

London, Pub. July 1st 1820 by Henry Colburn & Co. Conduit Street.

HISTORICAL AND CRITICAL ACCOUNT

OF

MR. MUDIE'S NATIONAL MEDALS.

No. I.

HIS MAJESTY GEORGE III.

A SERIES of National Medals cannot be more appropriately commenced than by devoting the first of that series to the Sovereign during whose reign the whole of those great events occurred which the remaining medals are intended to celebrate. He may, indeed, be justly considered as their source; for it was the policy he approved which created the opportunities for our naval and military heroes to signalise themselves. Had the monarch been other than he was, England, perhaps, would never have enrolled among her illustrious chiefs the names of Wellington, Nelson, Abercrombie, Howe, Moore, Duncan, Anglesea, and St. Vincent.

The reign of George the Third was not only the longest in the annals of England, but it was diversified with the most stupendous occurrences that ever marked the history of any country during a similar space of time. It cannot be attempted, on an occasion like the present, to trace even the outline of those great and multifarious events. They would require a space far more ample than we can pretend to assign to any one division of our labours. We shall confine ourselves, therefore, to an enumeration of the more prominent transactions — those which stand out with a bolder form, and define, as it were, the political character of the period alluded to.

George the Third ascended the throne in the midst of a war which, in 1763, was brought to a prosperous conclusion, and a general peace proclaimed. The youthful monarch early displayed his attachment to literature and the arts. In 1768 the Royal Academy was founded, and in the same year captain Cook, the illustrious circumnavigator of the globe, commenced those discoveries which have conferred so much fame upon the nautical enterprise of England. His Majesty's celebrated interviews with Dr. Johnson and Dr. Beattie, and the collecting of his magnificent library at Buckingham House, may be selected from among numerous proofs of his regard for those pursuits which more truly ennoble a nation than can ever be done by military glory.

In the year 1776 the American colonies, between whom and the mother-country angry disputes had long existed upon the subject of taxation, formally renounced their allegiance, and proclaimed themselves independent. Six years of an expensive and devastating war followed, before the British cabinet would consent to acknowledge their independence, and it was well known that his Majesty was the last to sanction the recognition. He was justly tenacious of possessions which descended to him with the crown he wore, and which it was his duty to preserve for his successor. This duty ceased to exist, only when success, in the contest, ceased to be possible, and when, consequently, a higher duty claimed his submission—that of relieving his people from the burden of a hopeless war.

The turbulent scenes of domestic politics that accompanied and succeeded this memorable struggle, the strife and the audacity of faction, and the final triumph of principles that must ever be identified with the constitution, belong to history. We pass them by, and hasten to record the next remarkable event which may be considered as personally connected with the Sovereign. We allude to the attempt upon his life on the 2d of August 1786 by a maniac of the name of Margaret Nicholson. His Majesty was alighting from his carriage at the garden gate of St. James's Palace, when she approached as if to present a paper which she held in her hand. The King was just in the act of taking it, when the maniac aimed a blow at his breast with a knife which she had concealed. His Majesty fortunately parried the thrust by a sudden movement of his body, and before she could repeat the meditated blow, one of the yeomen of the guard wrenched the weapon from her grasp. The natural benevolence of his Majesty's character signally manifested itself on this occasion; for the very first words he uttered to his attendants, and before he could know that insanity had prompted the deed, was, " do not hurt the poor woman." She was afterwards confined in Bethlehem Hospital.

Two years subsequently to this event, the King himself became the victim of that mental alienation which had directed the assassin's knife against his royal person. It was towards the end of autumn, in the year 1788, that the symptoms first displayed themselves. On the 24th of October he held a levee, where it was obvious to every one present that his health was seriously affected; but no suspicion of the real nature of the malady existed. On his return to Windsor the disorder assumed an alarming appearance, and by the beginning of November it was no longer possible to prevent the fatal intelligence from reaching the public ear. There was so little probability, in the judgment of his physicians, of his speedy recovery, that Parliament proceeded to discuss the necessary measures for establishing a regency. Happily, however, before these were completed, a communication was made to both Houses (on the 24th of February 1789) of his Majesty's entire recovery. The manifestations of public joy, in celebration of this auspicious event, were such as must have deeply convinced the King that he reigned in the hearts of an affectionate and loyal people.

Europe, at this period, was upon the verge of one of the most stupendous convulsions that ever agitated the frame of civil society. The French revolution was just beginning to raise its portentous head, — that revolution which, in its bloody and resistless course, spread devastation wherever it trod. When it first appeared above the political horizon, it was hailed, by many sincere worshippers, as the day-star of liberty. One man alone,—Edmund Burke,—saw, in its infant lineaments, those hideous features from which all Europe afterwards shrunk back aghast. He raised his warning voice, and prophesied of days that would come ; but he had worse than the fate of Cassandra, for his predictions were not only disbelieved when they were uttered ; they were denied also when they were fulfilled.

The firmness with which George the Third opposed himself to the torrent of infidelity, anarchy, and blood, which this revolution let loose upon Europe, forms the noblest quality of his political and personal character.   He embarked in the war with France, not from ambition, or from caprice, but from necessity, — that necessity which made it the duty of a Christian king, and the first magistrate of a free people, to take up arms for the defence of religion and liberty.   The nation gallantly supported their monarch; and if there be one thing more than another which should make us lament the solitude of his latter years, it is the reflection, that he was unconscious of the glorious issue which awaited the struggle he so nobly began.   It was the will of Providence, however, that it should be so.   He was permitted to see only the dawn of that regeneration for Europe which faintly appeared on her western boundary when the immortal Wellington planted his flag of triumph on the shores of Portugal.   In 1809 was fought the battle of Talavera, and in 1810 that fatal malady appeared which for ten long years withdrew him from all intercourse with his people.   The rest of his life became, indeed, a melancholy blank, during which the country knew little of its monarch, except that he lived. The monthly reports of his physicians told the same unvarying tale of unimpaired bodily health, but of unyielding mental alienation.   In this state of cheerless solitude, blind, insane, and latterly deaf, the royal sufferer continued to linger.   Three generations of his illustrious house descended to the tomb before him, as did likewise his venerable consort.   At length, however, nature gave way, and he himself yielded to that potent arm which vanquishes the mightiest of the sons of men with the same ease that it smites the weakest and most humble.   He expired on the 29th of January 1820, at Windsor Castle, at 35 minutes past eight o'clock in the evening.   He was in the 82d year of his age, and the 60th of his reign.

The character of George the Third is easily described.   It is merely necessary to tell what a man should be, and the picture is delineated.   In the practice of all those virtues which make private life lovely, he was exemplary.   As a husband, a father, a relative, and a friend, he not only rose superior to censure, but he was above calumny, which will dare to aim its envenomed shaft at sanctity itself.   Nor party rage, nor political animosity, nor disappointed ambition, nor baffled intrigue, was ever heard to breathe a whisper which could sully the blameless purity of his life. The virtues he delighted in were not those by which the vulgar admirers of kings are captivated; — it was in the endearing intercourse of private life that he appeared to most advantage. Pious, temperate, benevolent, unostentatious, he lived among us, and he ruled over us, above half a century, — the bright model of what a king, a Christian, and a man, should be.

A few days after his death the following expressive lines were written by an eminent public character, which form, at once, an accurate and appropriate eulogy. With these we shall conclude this article.

Chaste, pious, steadfast, merciful, and just, —
His pride, his people,—and his God, his trust;
To the third George approving Heaven ordain'd
A life unblemished, and a death unpain'd;
In goodness, greatness, years, his reign exceeds
Henry's mild life, and Edward's laurell'd deeds *.

DESCRIPTION OF THE MEDAL.

OBVERSE.—Head of the King, with this motto, " HOC AUSPICE ORBIS SALUS, 1817."—Mudie d. Webb f.

REVERSE.—Figures personifying Religion and Faith, or Honesty. These, in union with the rock behind the cornucopia and the rudder, imply that Religion, Integrity, and Constancy, have steered Britannia successfully through all her dangers up to the present period: marked on the exergue, 1817.

* This line alludes to the historical fact, that the three longest reigns in British history are those of three kings, each the third of their respective names,—Henry III. Edward III. and George III.

No. II.

SETTLEMENT OF THE BRITISH

AT

BOMBAY.

THE principal event which this Medal is intended to commemorate, is eminently national. Our empire in India has no parallel in ancient or modern history, and it would strike us as still more wonderful, were we but enabled to trace with precision its origin and progress. In these we discern that it has been the creature of circumstances. Commerce and war —the merchant and the soldier—have alternately developed that stupendous power which now seems consolidated beyond the influence of foreign aggression, or internal confederacy.

The discovery by Vasco de Gama of a passage to India by doubling the Cape of Good Hope, and the consequent influx of eastern treasures into Europe, excited the cupidity, and stimulated the enterprise, of all the maritime states. But the absurd pretensions which Portugal asserted, to an exclusive navigation of those seas, in consequence of that discovery by her adventurous commander, and the still more absurd deference which, for a time, was observed towards those arrogant pretensions, necessarily directed the attention of nautical and commercial men, to the practicability of exploring some other route to the eastern shores. Hence the many fruitless attempts, about the middle of the sixteenth century, to effect a passage to China, by a north-east or north-west passage.

At length, in 1577, Sir Francis Drake formed and executed the bold design of crossing the Pacific Ocean to India, and regaining England by the Cape of Good Hope. He was followed in 1586 by Cavendish, who performed the same hazardous navigation, and soon after the merchants of England began to devise means for carrying on a direct trade with the east by the Cape of Good Hope. This was towards the conclusion of the sixteenth century, when a certain number of merchants obtained a charter, and thus laid the foundations of the present East India Company. There was nothing in this charter, however, which distinguished it from the other charters of incorporation so commonly in that age bestowed upon trading associations. The progress which was subsequently made in establishing factories upon the Malabar coast, cannot with any propriety find a place in this descriptive sketch. We pass, therefore, to the particular event of which this Medal is intended to be the commemoration

In 1662 Charles II. espoused the Infanta, Catherine of Portugal, part of whose dowry was to be the cession of the island of Bombay to the King of England. A fleet of five men of war, commanded by the Earl of Marlborough, with five hundred troops, commanded by Sir Abraham Shipman, were sent to receive the possession. The armament arrived at Bombay on the 18th September 1662; but the governor evaded the cession. The English understood the treaty to include Salsette, and the other dependencies of Bombay. The Portuguese contended that the island of Bombay alone was to be relinquished, and the terms of the treaty were not sufficiently explicit to decide the question. It was refused, indeed, to surrender even Bombay, on the pretext that the letters or patent of the King did not accord with the usages of Portugal, and that therefore they must wait till further instructions were received. The Earl of Marlborough, having applied in vain, to the Company's President at Surat for assistance, resolved to return with the King's ships to England; but Sir Abraham Shipman, it was agreed, should land the troops on the island of Angedivah, twelve leagues distant from Goa.

On the arrival of the Earl of Marlborough in England, in 1663, the King remonstrated with the government of Portugal, when all intention of parting with the dependencies of Bombay was denied. The situation, in the mean time, of the troops at Angedivah, proved extremely unhealthy, and their numbers were greatly reduced by disease. This induced the commander to offer to the President and Council at Surat, to cede the King's rights to the Company. It need hardly be added, this offer was declined; for, in the first place, without the sanction of the King the cession would be invalid; and, in the next, the President and Council were too destitute of military resources to take possession of the place.

At length, after the death of Sir Abraham Shipman, and the greatest part of the troops, caused by famine and disease, Mr. Cooke, who succeeded to the command, determined to accept of Bombay, upon the terms prescribed by the Portuguese. When the knowledge of this convention reached England, the King refused to ratify it, as being contrary to the terms of his treaty with Portugal; but he sent out Sir Gervase Lucas to assume the government of the place. A few years experience, however, proved that the possession was more expensive than profitable, and it was again offered to the Company, by whom it was ultimately accepted. The grant bears date 1668. It was " to be held of the King in free and common soccage, as of the manor of East Greenwich, in the payment of the annual rent of £.10 in gold, on the 30th of September in each year." With the place was also given authority to exercise all political powers, necessary for its defence and government.

It remains to describe the particular event commemorated on the reverse of this medal.

The transitory peace of Amiens, and the causes which led to its rupture, need not be dwelt upon. Immediately, however, that it was known his Majesty had sent a message to Parliament, in the spring of 1803, announcing the probability of hostilities between the two countries, the French government dispatched intelligence of it to India. The transport which conveyed the news was intercepted by an English frigate, and carried to the English fleet, then lying before Pondicherry. The Governor-general of India, ignorant at that time of what was passing in Europe, gave immediate orders for her release, and she proceeded to her destination, which was to apprize Linois, the French Admiral who commanded in those seas, of the war likely soon to break out between England and France. Linois took the necessary precautions, upon receiving this information. He withdrew from Pondicherry, where, as we have already stated, the English fleet lay, and retired to the Isle of France. There he soon learnt, that declarations of war had been actually issued by the two governments at home, and rightly conjecturing that no advices upon the subject had reached any of the British presidencies in Hindostan, he prepared to avail himself of his exclusive information to the annoyance of our trade. He put to sea on a cruize, with six frigates, besides corvettes and other light vessels, and eight cutters armed in the country. With this fleet he made several valuable captures of our Indiamen, besides destroying, or compelling the English to destroy, at Bencoolen, a great many vessels.

Emboldened by these successes, he meditated a more lucrative enterprise. The China fleet attracted his cupidity, and joining with his own the Dutch force at Batavia, he put to sea again with a formidable fleet, consisting of the Marengo, of 80 guns; the Semillante and Belle Poule, of 44 each; a cutter and brigantine of 18, and a corvette of 28 guns. Thus prepared, he met, on the 13th of February 1804, our China ships, heavily and richly laden, under convoy of Capt. Dance of the Earl Camden, Indiaman. But the tempting prize, though within his view, was not within his grasp. The captains of the different vessels manifested no disposition to yield to the menacing and disproportionate force of Linois. That a fleet of mere merchantmen should thus attempt to dispute the mastery with one amply and expressly equipped for war, must have been a disagreeable surprise to the French Admiral. During four and twenty hours, he continued to manœuvre round them, and attempted to cut off part of the convoy. In this, however, he was not only frustrated, but he beheld his anticipated conquest suddenly assuming the offensive, and bearing down upon him in battle array. This they performed too in so gallant and decisive a manner, that he was compelled not only to forego his purpose, but to seek refuge at Batavia.

There are few exploits, even in the splendid annals of British naval heroism, more distinguished than this, and it well deserves the record here conferred upon it. It received at the time, not only the unanimous applause of the country, but some valuable tokens of approbation and gratitude were bestowed upon the captains and other officers, by the Committee of Merchants in London.—To Captain Dance was given a vase and a sword, each of £.100 value; and rewards of proportionate magnitude to the other officers, including the surgeons, pursers, mates, &c. The whole remuneration fell little short of £.50,000. But it should be recollected that the value of the fleet so gallantly preserved was estimated, by the supercargoes, including public and private investments, at upwards of eight millions sterling. Gratitude, therefore, may be supposed to have had some share in the munificent donations above mentioned, as well as admiration of the heroism which was displayed.

DESCRIPTION OF THE MEDAL.

OBVERSE.—The genius of the ocean planting the British flag or power at Bombay; which island is represented by a globe, and its fertility by a cornucopia. The Leopard is emblematical of India.

REVERSE.—The victory obtained by the East India Company's Merchant Ships over the French squadron, is here expressed by Neptune holding a figure of victory.

EARL HOWE.

THIS gallant Admiral was the third son of Sir Emanuel Scrope, second Lord Viscount Howe, and Mary Sophia Charlotte, eldest daughter to the Baron Kilmansegge. He was born in 1725, was educated at Eton, and entered the sea-service at the age of fourteen. He very early distinguished himself. In 1745, Lieutenant Howe was with Admiral Vernon in the Downs, but being raised to the rank of a Commander, in the Baltimore sloop of war, he joined the squadron then cruising off the coast of Scotland, and in an action which took place, gave a fine example of persevering intrepidity. The Baltimore, in company with another armed vessel, fell in with two French frigates of 30 guns, with troops and ammunition for the service of the Pretender, which she instantly attacked by running in between them. In the action which followed, captain Howe received a wound in his head, which at first appeared to be fatal. He soon discovered signs of life, however, and when the necessary operation was performed, he continued the action with redoubled spirit, and obliged the French ships, with their prodigious superiority of men and metal, to sheer off. His own ship was too much shattered to permit him to pursue them. His gallantry, on this occasion, caused him to be raised to the rank of a post captain.

In the interval between the years 1746 and 1757, he was actively engaged in his professional duties, in various parts of the world; but the detail of those services would be little interesting to the general reader. In the year 1757, a powerful fleet being prepared under the command of Sir Edward Hawke, to make an attack on the French coast, Captain Howe was appointed to the Magnanime, in which ship he battered the fort on the island of Aix, till it surrendered. In 1758 he was appointed the commodore of a small squadron which sailed to annoy the enemy on their coasts. This he effected with his usual success at St. Malo, where 100 sail of ships and several magazines were destroyed.

This expedition was soon followed by another, when Prince Edward, afterwards Duke of York, was entrusted to the care of commodore Howe, on board his ship the Essex. The fleet sailed on the 1st of August 1758, and on the 6th came to an anchor in the Bay of Cherburg, when the town was taken and the basin destroyed. The commodore next sailed to St. Malo; and as his instructions were to keep the coast of France in continual alarm, he very effectually obeyed them. The unsuccessful affair of St. Cas followed. Never were courage, skill, and humanity, however, more powerfully or more successfully displayed than on this occasion. He went in person in his barge, which was rowed through the thickest fire, to save the retreating soldiers; and the rest of the fleet, inspired by his conduct, followed his example. The consequence was, that at least 700 men were preserved, by his exertions, from the fire of the enemy or the fury of the waves.

In July of the same year, his elder brother, who was serving in America, found an early grave, and Commodore Howe succeeded to the titles and property of his family. In the following year (1759) Lord Howe was employed in the Channel, on board his old ship the Magnanime, but no opportunity for distinguishing himself occurred, till the month of November, when the French fleet, under Conflaus, was defeated. On his being presented to the King, after this victory, by Sir Edward Hawke, his Majesty said, " Your life, my Lord, has been one continued series of services to your country."

On the 23d of August 1763, his Lordship was appointed to the Board of Admiralty, where he remained till August 1765, when he was made treasurer of the navy. In October 1770 he was promoted to be rear-admiral of the blue, and commander-in-chief in the Mediterranean. In March 1775, he was appointed rear-admiral of the white, and in December of the same year, he was made vice-admiral of the blue. It was on one of these promotions that Lord Hawke, the first Lord of the Admiralty, rose in the House of Peers, and said, " I advised his Majesty to make the promotion. I have tried my Lord Howe on important occasions : he never asked me how he was to execute any important service, but always went and performed it."

In the course of the year 1778 Lord Howe was advanced to be vice-admiral of the white, and shortly after to the same rank in the red squadron. On the change of administration in 1782, he was created a Viscount of Great Britain, having been previously nominated admiral of the blue. He was then appointed to command the fleet fitted out for the relief of Gibraltar, and he ably fulfilled the important objects of the expedition. That fortress was effectually relieved, and the hostile fleet baffled, and dared, in vain, to battle. Peace was concluded shortly after, and in 1783 Lord Howe was promoted to the situation of first Lord of the Admiralty. This office he resigned, in the succeeding April, to Lord Keppel; but was re-appointed on the 30th of December in the same year. On the 24th of September 1787, he was advanced to the rank of admiral of the white; and in July 1788 he formally quitted his station at the Admiralty. In the following August he was created an Earl of Great Britain.

We now approach to the greatest exploit of his life, and which will transmit his name to posterity, among those naval heroes of England who have exalted her character as a great maritime state. On the breaking out of the revolutionary war in 1793, this gallant veteran, though then nearly 70 years of age, accepted the command of the Western squadron. During the first year in which he filled this high station, no very memorable occurrence took place, for the enemy would not shew themselves. But in the month of May 1794, the French being very anxious for the safety of a convoy daily expected from America, with an immense supply of corn and flour, naval stores, &c., the Brest fleet, under the command of Rear-Admiral Villaret, amounting to 26 sail of the line, ventured to sea. Lord Howe, being upon the look-out for the same convoy, went to sea with 25 ships of the line, and on the 28th of May descried the enemy to windward. After various previous manœuvres, which had been interrupted by a thick fog, the admiral found an opportunity of bringing the French to close action off Ushant, on the 1st of June. The ships bore up together for that purpose between seven and eight o'clock in the morning. Our fleet advanced in a close and compact line, and waited for the action, and sustained the attack with their customary resolution. "In less than an hour," we quote the gallant admiral's own dispatch, "after the close action commenced in the centre, the French admiral, engaged by the Queen Charlotte (Earl Howe's own ship), crowded off, and was followed by most of the ships in his van in a condition to carry sail after him." Ten, however, were so crippled, that they could not keep pace with the rest, but many of the British ships being also greatly damaged, some of the disabled vessels of the enemy effected their escape. Seven, however, remained in our possession, one of which (the Vengeur 74 guns) sunk almost immediately after being boarded as a prize. The remaining six were brought into Portsmouth, viz., two of 80, and four of 74 guns.

This victory, being the first which had been achieved since the commencement of the war, produced the liveliest sensations in the public mind. The victorious ships arrived safe in harbour with their prizes, and the admiral, officers, and crews, were received with every testimony of national gratitude. On the the 26th of the same month, their majesties, with some of the princesses arrived at Portsmouth, and proceeded the next morning in barges, to visit Lord Howe's ship, the Queen Charlotte, at Spithead. His Majesty held a naval levee on board, and presented the victorious admiral with a sword, enriched with diamonds, and a gold chain, with the naval medal suspended from it. The thanks of both Houses of Parliament, and the freedom of the city of London, followed the acknowledgments of the Sovereign.

This was the last naval enterprise in which the gallant veteran was engaged. It may be regarded, indeed, as the close, and a glorious close it was, of his professional life. He did not, however, retire wholly from the service, till the year 1797, when he finally resigned the command of the Western squadron. On the 2d of June, in that year he was invested with the insignia of the garter; and, on the 5th of August, 1799, his Lordship expired, at his house in Grafton Street, in the 74th year of his age. His death was occasioned by gout in the stomach. He left issue, three daughters, whom he had by his wife, the daughter of Chiverton Hartop, Esq. of Welby, in the county of Leicester. He married that lady in 1758. His daughters were, Lady Sophia Charlotte, married to the Hon. Pen. Ashton Curzon, eldest son of Lord Curzon, who died in 1797;

Lady Mary Indiana; and Lady Louisa Catherine, married to the Earl of Altamont in Ireland. He was succeeded in his Irish Viscounty by his brother, General Sir William Howe, who died in 1814; and in the English Barony by Lady Curzon.

DESCRIPTION OF THE MEDAL.

OBVERSE.—Head of Admiral Earl Howe, by Wyon.

REVERSE.—As the victory over the French, off Ushant, was the first in the late war, a general representation of the triumphant superiority of the British flag on the ocean, is here represented by Neptune actively directing the successes of the British by sea.

D

No. IV.

EARL ST. VINCENT.

JOHN JERVIS, Earl St. Vincent, was born January 9, 1734, and is still living, being now in his eighty-seventh year. He is descended from an ancient and respectable family in Staffordshire; and is the second and youngest son of Swynfen Jervis, Esq. barrister at law, counsel to the Admiralty, and auditor of Greenwich Hospital. His mother was the sister of Sir Thomas Parker, Lord Chief Baron of the Exchequer, and daughter of George Parker, of Park Hall, County of Stafford.

At the early period of ten years of age his Lordship quitted Burton Grammar School, where he was educated, and entered into the navy. His first service was on board the Gloucester of 50 guns, sent on the Jamaica station with the broad pendant of the Hon. George Townshend.

On the 19th February 1755, he was raised to the rank of lieutenant, and shortly after accompanied Sir Charles Saunders in the expedition sent against Quebec, at the commencement of the seven years' war. He acquitted himself so much to the satisfaction of this commander, that he was, at no great distance of time, appointed to the Porcupine sloop. On the 13th October 1768, he was promoted to the rank of post captain, and to the command of the Gosport of 40 guns, in which he continued till the end of the war.

In 1774 Captain Jervis was promoted to the Foudroyant, an 84 gun ship, originally belonging to the French, but taken from them in 1754. In the memorable engagement between the French and British fleets, on the 27th and 28th of July 1778, his Lordship commanded this ship, which was as closely engaged, and as much disabled, as any one in the fleet.

We come now to mention " one of the most brilliant actions that had occurred during the American war," to use the words of Admiral Barrington. In April 1782 the ministry had intelligence that a French armament was ready for sea at Brest, and destined for the East Indies.

A suitable squadron was ordered out on the occasion, under the command of Vice Admiral Barrington, in order to intercept the enemy, and the success of the expedition was greatly owing to the activity and judgment of Captain Jervis. The Admiral set sail for the Bay of Biscay, and when a short distance off Ushant, Captain Mc Bride, commanding the Artois, which was very far a-head, made the signal for discovering an enemy's fleet. In consequence of this, the Admiral hove out the signal for a general chace, and about three o'clock the enemy became visible; but the Admiral's ship was left very far astern by many of the prime sailing ships. Among these the Foudroyant, Captain Jervis, so far outstripped the rest, that when night came on, with hazy weather, he soon lost them entirely, but still kept a full view of the enemy, whom he pursued with unremitting vigor. The chased fleet consisted of 18 sail, and were under the protection of the Protecteur and Pegase of 74 guns each, the Actionnaire of 64 guns, and a frigate. The Foudroyant gained so fast upon the chace, that it was evident they could not escape without an engagement; the convoy was therefore dispersed by signal, and the two French seventy-fours having consulted together, it was determined that, as the Protecteur had a large quantity of money on board, she should make the best of her way, and if fighting was inevitable the Pegase was to abide the consequence. A little before one A. M. the Foudroyant came up, and was closely engaged with the Pegase, commanded by the Chevalier de Sillans. The action was extremely fierce, while it lasted; but in less than an hour Captain Jervis laid the Pegase aboard on the larboard quarter, and she was compelled to strike, though she carried 74 guns and 700 men. On board the Pegase, eighty were killed and wounded, and the hull, masts, and yards materially injured; while the Foudroyant sustained but little injury, and not a man was killed, and only two or three slightly wounded. Captain Jervis was among the latter, having been struck by a splinter on the temple. In consequence of this gallant action Captain Jervis was honoured with the insignia of Knight of the Bath. About this period he was married to his first cousin Miss Parker, and daughter of Sir Thomas Parker.

In the year 1787, Sir John Jervis was promoted to the rank of the rear-admiral of the blue, and in the year 1790 to that of rear-admiral of the white.

At the breaking out of the French war in 1793, he was appointed to command the squadron destined to co-operate with Sir C. Grey in the reduction of the French West India Islands. In this toilsome service he acquitted himself with the highest honor to himself, and benefit to the country. His health, however, suffered severely from the climate, and he was obliged to return home, but not until the expedition had accomplished the objects for which it was dispatched. After four months' repose, he was ordered to succeed Admiral Hotham in the command of the Mediterranean squadron, where he blocked up the Spanish fleet, and bombarded Cadiz.

On the 1st June 1796, he was promoted to the rank of admiral of the blue.

We have now arrived at the period when he achieved that memorable victory which places his name by the side of the greatest naval heroes that England has produced. We have already stated that he was commanding the Mediterranean squadron, where he had to watch not only the Toulon fleet, but the movement of the Spaniards in Cadiz. On the 6th February 1797, Rear Admiral Parker joined him with a reinforcement from England; but still he had to contend with an enemy far superior in point of numbers.

On the 13th of February at night, Captain Foote of the Niger informed the admiral that the Spanish squadron was not more than three or four leagues distant, and at day-break on the 14th the two fleets were in complete order of battle, off Cape St. Vincent. The Spanish fleet was commanded by Don Juan de Cordova, and consisted of 27 sail of the line, one of which was a four decker, and mounted 136 guns; six were three deckers of 112 guns each; two of 84 guns; and eighteen of 74. The British squadron amounted only to fifteen sail of the line, four frigates, a sloop of war, and a cutter. Of these, six were three deckers, eight were of 74 guns, and one of 64.

When the two fleets hove in sight of each other, some of the enemy's ships appeared to be separated from the main body. The British admiral instantly conceived the design of cutting these off before they could rejoin, or the main body arrive to their assistance ; but, observing the position of the main body, he formed his fleet into a line of battle a-head and a-stern, and about half past eleven signified his intention to push through the enemy's line. The signal was accordingly made for action. His Lordship accomplished his design, and a part of the fleet was most effectually separated from the main body, which was in consequence reduced to eighteen sail of the line. Towards this main body the British admiral now directed his attention. He again made the signal for passing through the enemy's line, which the Spanish commander endeavoured to counteract, by wearing round the rear of the British line, to join his ships to leeward. This manœuvre, however, was baffled by Commodore Nelson, who boldly placed himself along side the Santissima Trinidada, of 136 guns, though his own ship, the Captain, mounted only 74. Although the Santissima Trinidada was assisted by her two seconds, both three deckers, the intrepid Nelson did not shrink from the unequal contest. Happily, the Culloden and Blenheim pressed to his assistance, and the approach of Admiral Parker, with four other ships of the line, decisively frustrated the design of the Spanish admiral, of rejoining his ships to leeward.

The advantage now lay completely with the British, and the Spanish fleet was beginning to crowd off, when, in the confusion of their retreat, some of them doubled on each other. Admiral Jervis then bore up with his division, consisting of seven ships, intending to rake the enemy in succession ; but not being able to effect this he ordered the leading ship, the Excellent, to bear up, while he, in the Victory, passed to leeward of the rearmost ships of the enemy. Captain Collingwood, who commanded the Excellent, accordingly passed between the two rearmost ships of the Spaniards, and poured such an effectual broadside into the San Ysidro, that she was obliged to submit.

After this, the Excellent moved on to the relief of the Captain, which was engaged with a three decker ; but before she could arrive, this ship got foul of her second, a two decker, in which state they were both boarded by the Captain, and the maller, the San Nicholas, was speedily taken possession of. The three decker, the San Josef, also surrendered, and became a prize to Commodore Nelson, who headed the party which boarded her from the San Nicholas. In the mean time Admiral Jervis, who had ordered the Victory to be laid aside the Salvator del Mundo, poured in such an effectual fire, that she struck almost immediately.

Thus, four of the enemy's ships were captured by the British, whose loss in killed and wounded was exactly 300 men; while that of the Spaniards, in the captured ships alone, amounted to 693. The remainder of the Spanish fleet then took shelter in Cadiz, and Sir John Jervis soon after entered the Tagus with his fleet and prizes, amid the cheering shouts of the populace.

For this signal service to his country he received the thanks of both Houses of Parliament, and was elevated to the peerage (May 27th, 1797) by the titles of Earl St. Vincent, and Baron Jervis of Meaford. He also received a gold medal, and a pension of £.3000 per annum.

In politics, the noble Earl has generally acted with the Whigs; but though thus opposed to the government, he never found that his promotion was obstructed, or his professional merits neglected.

In 1801, when Mr. Pitt retired from the administration, Earl St. Vincent accepted the office of first Lord of the Admiralty, under the new ministry. This situation he retained till Mr. Pitt's return to power in 1804. We abstain from any remarks upon the circumstances that took place during the time he presided over the naval affairs of the country.

DESCRIPTION OF THE MEDAL.

OBVERSE.—Admiral Earl St. Vincent, by Mills, from a bust by Chantrey.

REVERSE.—The genius of war hurling the destruction of the British fire on the Spanish Fleet, off Cape St. Vincent.

V

VI

VII

VIII

Normand filit.

London Pub. July 1.st 1820, by Henry Colburn & C.º Conduit Street.

LORD DUNCAN.

THIS distinguished naval officer was the second son of Alexander Duncan, esq. of Lundie, in the county of Angus, Scotland, and was born in the month of July 1731. He received the rudiments of his education at Dundee, and seems to have been early intended for the sea, for in 1746, when he was only fifteen years old, he was put under Captain Haldane, at that time commander of the Shoreham frigate, and with whom he continued two or three years.

The history of his life, down to that period which afforded him the opportunity of conspicuously signalising himself as a great naval commander, contains little that can deserve to be recorded. It differs, indeed, in no respect from that of any other captain in the British navy, or rather, it may be described as having been less than ordinarily fertile of those incidents which commonly diversify a nautical career. This, no doubt, must be ascribed to the peculiarity of his situation; for it is impossible to suppose, that the talents which shone forth with so much lustre in the evening of his life would not have blazed with equal or superior brightness in its meridian, had there existed opportunities for their display. But, in fact, it is with the navy as with every other profession;—while one man, by a fortunate concurrence of circumstances, starts into fame, there are hundreds who, under similar circumstances, would become equally illustrious.

It may be satisfactory, however, briefly to mark the gradations by which Lord Duncan attained to the high professional rank which he enjoyed.

In February 1761 he was made a post-captain, and appointed to the Valiant of 74 guns, nor did he receive any other promotion in the long interval which elapsed between that period and the year 1789. During all that time, however, he was actively employed, and participated in most of the naval actions which occurred while the country was at war.

On the 14th of September 1789 he was promoted to be rear-admiral of the blue, and on the 22d of September 1790 he attained the same rank in the white squadron. On the 1st of February 1793 he was made vice-admiral of the blue; vice-admiral of the white, April 12, 1794; admiral of the blue, June 1, 1795; and lastly, admiral of the white, Feb, 14, 1799.

It was in the year 1795 he received the appointment which laid the foundation for that gallant achievement which will carry his name down to posterity. He was nominated commander-in-chief in what is called the North Seas, the limits of his command extending from the North Foreland as far north as the operations of the enemy he was sent to encounter might render necessary. He accordingly hoisted his flag on board the Prince George of 98 guns, at Chatham; but that ship being considered too large for the particular quarter in which the Admiral was intended to act, he removed soon afterwards into the Venerable of 74 guns, and proceeded to carry into execution the very important trust which was confided to him. Above two years, however, elapsed before any thing occurred beyond the ordinary routine of such a service; but the vigilance and activity of Admiral Duncan during that period were eminently serviceable. Not only were numerous small captures made, and the Dutch trade almost annihilated, but the fleet belonging to the United Provinces, though consisting of fifteen ships of the line, six frigates, and five sloops of war, was obliged to remain quietly in port, or, at most, to indulge itself only in short trips to sea when the British were compelled, from want of water and provisions, to repair to their own coasts for a few days.

It was at this period (June 1797) that the mutiny broke out in the navy, and threatened the most awful consequences to the country. In Admiral Duncan's squadron it raged with so much fury that he was left with only three ships to watch the enemy. Still, however, he remained firm in his position at the Texel, and succeeded in keeping the Dutch fleet from proceeding to sea. What were his own conduct and feelings at this trying moment will be best understood from the following piece of artless and affecting oratory, which to be admired needs only to be read. Having assembled his crew, who had not swerved from their duty, on the quarter-deck, he thus addressed them : — " My lads, I once more call you together, with a sorrowful heart from what I have long seen of the disaffection of the fleets ; I call it *disaffection*, for the crews have no *grievances*. To be deserted by my fleet, in the face of an enemy, is a disgrace which I believe never before happened to a British admiral ; nor could I have supposed it. My greatest comfort, under God, is, that I have been supported by the officers, seamen, and marines of *this ship*, for which, with a heart overflowing with gratitude, I request you to accept my sincere thanks. It has often been my pride, with you, to look into the Texel, and see a foe which dreaded coming out to meet us. My pride is *now* humbled indeed. My feelings are not easily to be expressed. Our cup has overflowed, and made us wanton. The all-wise Providence has given us this check as a warning, and I hope we shall profit by it. On HIM then let us trust, where our only security can be found."—The crew were so affected by this impressive address, that, on retiring, there was not a dry eye among them.

On the suppression of the mutiny, the Admiral resumed his station with his whole fleet off the coast of Holland; but after a long and very vigilant attention, he was compelled to repair to Yarmouth Roads to refit. The Batavian commander seized that opportunity, and put to sea. Captain Sir H. Trollope, however, who was upon the look-out, having discovered the enemy, dispatched a vessel with the glad intelligence to Admiral Duncan, who immediately set sail, and on the 11th of October 1797 fell in with Captain Trollope's squadron of observation, with a signal flying for an enemy to the leeward. By a masterly manœuvre the Admiral placed himself between them and the Texel, so as to prevent them from re-entering without risking an engagement. An action accordingly ensued between Camperdown and Egmont, in nine fathoms water, and within five miles of the coast. The battle was sustained with great gallantry on both sides ; the Admiral's own ship, in pursuance of a plan of naval evolution upon which he had long before determined, broke the enemy's line, and closely engaged the Dutch Admiral, De Winter, who, after a noble defence, was compelled to strike. In the whole, nine ships of the line were captured ; and, taking all things into consideration, the time of the year, the force of the enemy, and the nearness to a dangerous shore, this

E

action may be regarded as one of the most brilliant that graces our naval annals.

The honours which were conferred upon the venerable Admiral received the approbation of all parties. He was created Lord Viscount Duncan, of Camperdown, and Baron Duncan of Dundee in the shire of Perth. A pension of £.2000 a year was also granted his Lordship for himself and the two next heirs of the peerage. On his being introduced into the House of Peers on the 8th of November, the Lord Chancellor communicated to him the thanks of the House, and in his speech said,—" He congratulated his Lordship upon his accession to the honour of a distinguished seat in that place, to which his meritorious and *unparalleled* professional conduct had deservedly raised him !"

His Lordship, after this victory, continued to retain the same command until the year 1800, when, in consequence of his great age, he withdrew from active service. He did not, however, long survive his retirement, for on the 4th of August 1804 he died at his seat in Scotland. He had married, in June 1777, Henrietta, daughter of the late Right Hon. Robert Dundas, Lord President of the Court of Session in Scotland, and elder brother of Lord Melville, by whom he had a large family. He was succeeded in his titles and estates by Robert, his second son.

DESCRIPTION OF THE MEDAL.

OBVERSE. — Head of Admiral Lord Duncan, of masterly execution, by Webb. Inscription, " ADM. VISCOUNT DUNCAN."

REVERSE. — Admiral De Winter's surrender of his sword to the British Admiral, on the memorable defeat of the Dutch, off Camperdown. Dutch fleet defeated, nine ships of the line captured, 11th Oct. 1797. — Mudie direxit. W. Wyon fecit.

ADMIRAL LORD NELSON.

THIS illustrious naval hero was born on the 29th September, 1758, in the parsonage house of Burnham Thorpe, a village in the county of Norfolk, of which his father, the Rev. Edmund Nelson, was rector. His mother's maiden name was Catharine Suckling, and her grandmother was an elder sister of Sir Robert Walpole. Horatio Nelson was named after his godfather, the first Lord Walpole. Mrs. Nelson died in 1767, leaving eight out of eleven children.

The young Horatio commenced his naval education under the tuition of his maternal uncle, Captain Maurice Suckling, who then commanded the Raisonnable. It was his own choice that fixed him in this profession; for, being of a delicate constitution, his father would doubtless have preferred some less severe and less laborious pursuit. When he wrote to Captain Suckling on the subject, "what," he inquired in reply, " has poor Horatio done, who is so weak, that he, above all the rest, should be sent to rough it out at sea? But let him come, and the first time we go into action, a cannon ball may knock off his head, and provide for him at once."

He accordingly joined his uncle's ship, but it having been commissioned only on account of the dispute then subsisting respecting the Falkland Islands, it was paid off as soon as that dispute was adjusted, and Captain Suckling was removed to the Triumph 74, then stationed as a guardship in the Thames. Young Nelson now made a voyage to the West Indies in a merchant ship, and upon his return in July 1772, again joined the Triumph, on board of which he had not been many months when his love of enterprize was excited by hearing that two ships were fitting out for a voyage of discovery towards the North Pole.

This expedition was to be commanded by the Hon. Captain Constantine John Phipps, eldest son of Lord Mulgrave. The Race Horse and

Carcass bombs were selected as the strongest ships for this hazardous enterprise, and after much difficulty (it being determined to take out only effective men, instead of the usual number of boys) young Nelson obtained the humble appointment of a cockswain on board the latter, which was commanded by Captain Lutwidge. The expedition sailed from the Nore on the 4th June 1773.

It does not fall within the scope of this work to relate the progress of this voyage of discovery; but an anecdote connected with the future hero of England may be recorded.

One night, during the midwatch, he stole from the ship with one of his comrades, taking advantage of a rising fog, and set out over the ice in pursuit of a bear. It was not long before they were missed. The fog thickened, and Captain Lutwidge and his officers became exceedingly alarmed for their safety. Between three and four in the morning the weather cleared, and the two adventurers were seen at a considerable distance from the ship, attacking a huge bear. The signal for them to return was immediately made. Nelson's comrade called upon him to obey it, but in vain. His musket had flashed in the pan; their ammunition was expended; and a chasm in the ice which divided him from the bear probably preserved his life. "Never mind" he cried, "do but let me get a blow at this devil with the but-end of my musket, and we shall have him." Captain Lutwidge, however, seeing his danger, fired a gun, which had the effect of frightening the beast; and the boy then returned somewhat afraid of the consequences of his trespass. The captain reprimanded him sternly for conduct so unworthy of the office which he filled, and desired to know what motive he could have for hunting a bear. "Sir," said he, pouting his lip, as he was wont to do when agitated, "I wished to kill the bear, that I might carry the skin to my father."

When the ships returned to England, they were paid off, and Nelson, by the recommendation of his uncle, was placed with Captain Farmer of the Sea Horse of 20 guns, then going out to the East Indies, in the squadron under Sir Edward Hughes. When he had been about eighteen months in India, he felt the effects of that climate, so perilous to European constitutions, and would certainly have sunk into an early grave, had he not immediately returned to England.

The gradations by which he subsequently rose to various commands in the British navy cannot be minutely traced in this sketch of his professional career; neither can we attempt to delineate the incidents of his private life. They must be sought in a distinct biography of the illustrious hero. It will be enough for our purpose to exhibit him at that advanced period, when his fame was brightening into splendor, and when he was upon the eve of performing those great exploits which have enrolled his name not only among the most consummate commanders of his own country, but have ranked him with the most renowned of the age in which he lived. This will be more suited to our purpose than a dry catalogue of the different frigates he commanded, or a barren chronology of the periods when he was promoted in the service. It should be observed, however, that in whatever station he filled, whether as midshipman, lieutenant, or captain, he gave unequivocal proofs of that skill, intrepidity, and promptitude which he afterwards so pre-eminently displayed on more important occasions. We cannot detail these distinguished services with more brevity, or more simplicity, than was done by the hero himself, in the following memorial to his Sovereign. After the battle off Cape St. Vincent, which was fought by Sir John Jervis, in February 1797, and in which Nelson, then Commodore Nelson, bore a distinguished part, it was proposed to bestow on him a pension of £.1,000 a year; but etiquette required that he should give in a memorial of his services. He accordingly presented the following one, which, to use the words of his biographer, " like the general course of his wonderful life, has no parallel in naval history."

" To the King's Most Excellent Majesty:
The Memorial of Sir Horatio Nelson, K. B., and a Rear Admiral in your Majesty's fleet:

" That during the present war your Memorialist has been in *four* actions with the fleets of the enemy, *viz.* on the 13th and 14th of March 1795; on the 13th of July 1795; and on the 14th February 1797; in *three* actions with frigates; in *six* engagements against batteries; in *ten* actions in boats employed in cutting out of harbours, in destroying vessels, and in taking three towns. Your Memorialist has also served on

shore with the army four months, and commanded the batteries at the
sieges of Bastia and Calvi.

" That during the war he has assisted at the capture of *seven* sail of
the line, *six* frigates, *four* corvettes, and *eleven* privateers of different
sizes; and taken and destroyed nearly *fifty* sail of merchant vessels; and
your Memorialist has actually been engaged against the enemy upwards
of ONE HUNDRED AND TWENTY TIMES.

" In which services, your Memorialist has lost his right eye and arm,
and been severely wounded and bruised in his body. All of which services and wounds your Memorialist most humbly submits to your Majesty's
most gracious consideration.

  October 1797.   HORATIO NELSON."

At this period he had not attained his fortieth year, and yet such was
the career of glory and of peril which he had seen ! Had he never afterwards stepped on a quarter deck, his services would have transcended
those of any naval hero which this country has produced. But he was
still destined to perform, what he alone could perform, deeds that surpassed
all he had hitherto achieved. It is these which the medal accompanying
this description, is chiefly intended to commemorate.

Early in the year 1798 Sir Horatio Nelson hoisted his flag in the Vanguard, and immediately on his rejoining Earl St. Vincent, he was dispatched, with a small squadron to the Mediterranean, to ascertain, if
possible, the object of the great expedition which at that time was fitting out under Buonaparte at Toulon. The defeat of this armament,
whatever might be its destination, was deemed, by the British government, an object paramount to every other. After a variety of untoward
accidents, which enabled the French fleet to put to sea, Nelson learned
that the enemy had surprised Malta. Thither he immediately prepared
to follow, and had formed a plan for attacking them while at Gozo; but,
on the 22d of June intelligence reached him that they had left that island
on the 16th, the day after their arrival. He then pursued them to
Egypt. When he reached Alexandria, however, the enemy were not
there. Baffled in his object, he returned to Sicily, took in stores at Syra-
cuse, and afterwards made for the Morea. There, on the 28th July he
learnt that the French had been seen, about a month before, steering to

the S. E. from Candia. He immediately steered again for the coast of Egypt. On the first of August they came in sight of Alexandria, and at four in the afternoon Captain Hood of the Zealous made signal for the French fleet. For many preceding days Nelson had hardly taken either sleep or food. He now ordered his dinner to be served, while preparations were making for battle; and when his officers rose from table, and went to their separate stations, he said to them, " Before this time to-morrow I shall have gained a peerage or Westminster Abbey."

The French fleet consisted of 13 ships of the line and 4 frigates, carrying 1196 guns, and 11,230 men. The English had the same number of ships of the line, and one 50 gun ship, carrying 1,012 guns and 8,068 men. The English ships were all seventy-fours; the French had three 80 gun ships, and one three decker of 120.

Admiral Brueys, not being able to enter the port of Alexandria, which time and neglect had ruined, moored his ships in Aboukir Bay in a strong and compact line of battle; the headmost vessel, according to his own account, being as close as possible to a shoal on the N. W., and the rest of the fleet forming a kind of curve along the line of deep water, so as not to be turned by any means in the S. W. The commissary of the fleet said they were moored in such a manner as to bid defiance to a force more than double their own.

The moment Nelson perceived the position of the French, that intuitive genius with which he was endowed displayed itself; and it instantly struck him, that where there was room for an enemy's ship to swing, there was room for one of ours to anchor. The plan which he intended to pursue, therefore, was, to keep entirely on the outer side of the French line, and station his ships, as far as he was able, one on the outer bow, and another on the outer quarter of each of the enemy's. Captain Berry when he comprehended the scope of the design, exclaimed with transport, " If we succeed, what will the world say ?"—" There is no *if* in the case, "replied the admiral; " that we shall succeed is certain; who may live to tell the story is a very different question."

The action commenced at sun-set. About half past six o'clock the Goliath, Captain Foley, and the Zealous, Captain Hood, received the first fire from the enemy. A profound silence prevailed through the whole fleet. On board every one of the British ships, the crews were employed in making ready for anchoring. The shores of the Bay of Aboukir were lined with spectators, who watched the approach of the English fleet, and the impending conflict, with trembling awe and astonishment. While the advanced ships doubled the French line, the Vanguard, with Nelson himself on board, was the first that anchored on the outer side of the enemy within half pistol shot of their third ship, the Spartiate. Nelson had six colours flying in different parts of his rigging lest they should be shot away. That they should be struck, no British admiral considers as a possibility.

The two first ships of the French line were dismasted within a quarter of an hour after the commencement of the action; and the others had suffered so severely, that victory was already certain. The third, fourth, and fifth were taken possession of at half past eight. Meanwhile, Nelson received a severe wound on the head from a piece of langridge shot. Captain Berry caught him in his arms as he was falling. The great effusion of blood which ensued occasioned an apprehension that the wound was mortal. Nelson himself thought so. A large flap of the skin of the forehead, cut from the bone, had fallen over one eye, and the other being blind, he was in total darkness. When, however, the surgeon came to examine his wound, he found that it was merely superficial. He ordered him to remain quiet, but Nelson could not rest. He began to write dispatches, when suddenly a cry was heard on the deck that the Orient was on fire. To the astonishment of every one, Nelson appeared on the quarter deck, and was busily employed in giving orders that boats should be sent for the relief of the enemy. It was soon after nine that the fire on board the Orient broke out. Brueys, the French admiral was dead. He had received three wounds, yet would not leave his post. A fourth cut him almost in two. About ten the ship blew up. The explosion was tremendous, and was followed by an awful silence. The firing instantly ceased on both sides! The pause, thus produced, was at once solemn and sublime.

The battle re-commenced with the ships to the leeward of the centre, and continued till about three. At day-break, the two rear ships of the enemy were the only ships of the line that had their colours flying. They cut their cables in the forenoon, not having been engaged, and stood out to sea, and two frigates with them. The Zealous pursued; but as there was no other ship in a condition to support captain Hood, he was recalled. These, however, were all that escaped, and the victory was the most complete and glorious in the annals of naval history. Of thirteen sail of the line, nine were taken, and two burnt: of the four frigates, one was sunk, and another, the Artemise, was burnt by her captain, who escaped with most of his crew to shore. The British loss in killed and wounded amounted to 895. Westcott was the only captain who fell. Of the French, 3105, including the wounded, were sent on shore, by cartel; and 5225 perished.

Nelson was now at the summit of his glory. Congratulations, rewards and honours were showered upon him by all the states and princes and powers, to whom his victory gave a respite. He was created Baron Nelson of the Nile and of Burnham Thorpe, with a pension of £.2,000 for his own life and those of his two immediate successors. A grant of £.10,000 was voted to him by the East India Company; the Turkish Company presented him with a piece of plate; and the City of London bestowed upon him a magnificent sword.

We pass now to the next great exploit commemorated by this medal.

Nelson returned to England in November 1800; and in January 1801 he received orders to embark again. He was now raised to the rank of vice-admiral of the blue, and soon after hoisted his flag on board the San Josef of 112 guns, his own prize at the battle off Cape St. Vincent. About this time the Emperor Paul in Russia had renewed the Northern confederacy, the express and avowed object of which was to set limits to the naval supremacy of England. A resolution being taken by the English Cabinet to attempt its dissolution, a formidable fleet was fitted out for the North seas, under Sir Hyde Parker, in which Lord Nelson consented to go second in command. Having shifted his flag to the St. George of 98 guns, he sailed with the fleet in the month of March. On the 30th of that month he led the way through the Sound, which was passed without any loss.

The battle of Copenhagen, though less splendid in its character, and certainly less important in its consequences, than the battle of the Nile,

F

presented an ample opportunity for the display of Nelson's warlike genius. The Danes were well prepared for defence. Upwards of two hundred pieces of cannon were mounted upon the crown batteries at the entrance of the harbour, and a line of 25 two deckers, frigates, and floating batteries was moored across its mouth. An attack being determined on, the conduct of it was entrusted to Lord Nelson. The action was fought on the 2d of April 1801. It began about 10 o'clock in the morning, and was as terrible a conflict as any upon record. Nelson himself acknowledged, that even he had never been in a more perilous engagement. While he was pacing the quarter deck, a shot through the main mast knocked the splinters about. "It is warm work," he observed, to an officer, smiling, " and this day may be the last to any of us in a moment; but mark you," added he, with strong emotion, "I would not be elsewhere for thousands!" The commander-in-chief, Sir Hyde Parker, after the battle had raged for three hours, began to despair of success, and he ordered the signal for recal to be made. Nelson would not notice it. "You know Foley," said he, turning to the captain, "I have only one eye, I have a right to be blind sometimes;" and then, putting the glass to his blind eye, in that mood of mind which sports with bitterness, he exclaimed, "I really do not see the signal." Immediately after, he said, "keep mine for closer battle flying! That is the way I answer such signals! Nail mine to the mast!" About two o'clock, great part of the Danish line had ceased to fire, and victory was no longer doubtful. But it was difficult to take possession of the vanquished ships, on account of the firing which was still kept up from the shore. These ships lay between the English fleet and the land batteries, and the fire from each was equally destructive to the poor devoted Danes. Nelson, who was as humane as he was brave, was shocked at this massacre, for such he called it; and, with a presence of mind peculiar to himself, he retired into the stern gallery and wrote thus to the Crown Prince: " Vice-Admiral Lord Nelson has been commanded to spare Denmark, when she no longer resists. The line of defence which covered her shores has struck to the British flag; but if the firing is continued on the part of Denmark, he must set on fire all the prizes he has taken, without having the power of saving the men who have so nobly defended them. The brave Danes are the brothers, and should never be the enemies of the English." This energetic appeal led to a conference, which finally ended in a treaty, and the Northern confederacy was anni-hilated.

It was a murderous action. Our loss, in killed and wounded, was 953. The loss of the Danes, including prisoners, amounted to about 6,000.

For the battle of Copenhagen Nelson was raised to the rank of a Vis-count.

We now approach the closing scene of his glory, the battle of Trafalgar, which was fought on the 21st of October 1805. The French and Spanish fleets lay at anchor in the Bay of Cadiz, waiting for a favourable wind to put to sea. Nelson arrived off Cadiz on the 29th of September, his birth day. On that same day, Villeneuve, who commanded the combined squadron, received orders to sail the first opportunity; but when he heard that Nelson had resumed the command, he called a council of war, and it was determined not to leave Cadiz, unless they had reason to believe them-selves stronger, by one third, than the British force. Nelson did not remain directly off Cadiz with his fleet, nor even within sight of the port. His object was to induce the enemy to come out, and in this he at length succeeded. Relying on their own superiority, they put to sea on the 19th of October, and on the 21st he intercepted them off Trafalgar, about sixty miles east of Cadiz. Our fleet consisted of 27 sail of the line and four frigates : theirs of 33 and seven large frigates. Their superiority was greater in size and weight of metal than in numbers. They had four thousand troops on board, and the best riflemen who could be procured. Many of them were Tyrolese. Signal was made to bear down on the enemy in two lines, and the fleet set all sail. Admiral Collingwood in the Royal Sovereign led the lee line of thirteen ships; the Victory, on board of which was Nelson himself, led the weather line of fourteen.

Villeneuve was a skilful seaman. His plan of defence was as well con-ceived, and as original, as the plan of attack. He formed the fleet in a double line, every alternate ship being about a cable's length to windward of her second a-head and a-stern.

Nelson felt certain of a triumphant issue to the day, and just before the action commenced he asked captain Blackwood if he did not think there was a signal wanting. Captain Blackwood answered that he thought the whole fleet seemed very clearly to understand what they were about. "These words," says the biographer of Nelson, " were scarcely spoken before that signal was made which will be remembered as long as the language, or even the memory of England shall endure—Nelson's last signal :—" ENGLAND EXPECTS EVERY MAN TO DO HIS DUTY !" It · was received throughout the fleet with a shout of answering acclamation, made sublime by the spirit which it breathed, and the feeling which it expressed. "Now," said Nelson, "I can do no more. We must trust to the great disposer of all events, and the justice of our cause. I thank God for this great opportunity of doing my duty !"

The battle began at ten minutes before twelve. The French admiral, from the Bucentaure, beheld the new manner in which his enemy was advancing, Nelson and Collingwood each leading his line, and, pointing them out to his officers, he is said to have exclaimed, that such conduct could not fail to be successful. Nelson wore, on this memorable day, his admiral's frock coat, bearing on the left breast four stars, of the different orders with which he was invested. It was feared, and too truly, that these conspicuous badges of his past glory would render him an obvious mark for the enemy, who, it was well known, had riflemen on board their vessels. His officers consulted among themselves upon the propriety of suggesting this to him, though they knew any request to change his dress, or cover his stars, would highly displease him. " In honour I gained them," he exclaimed, when such a thing had been hinted to him formerly, " and in honour I will die with them." Mr. Beatty, his surgeon, had resolved, however, to risk his displeasure, but he was ordered from the quarter-deck before he could find an opportunity of speaking to him.

Nelson's column was steered about two points more to the north than Collingwood's, in order to cut off the enemy's escape into Cadiz. They continued to fire a gun at a time at the Victory, till they saw that a shot had passed through her main top-gallant sail, and they then opened their broadsides, aiming chiefly at her rigging, in the hope of disabling her before she could close with them. Nelson, as usual, had hoisted several flags, lest one should be shot away. The enemy shewed no colours till late in the action, when they began to feel the necessity of having them to strike. For this reason the Santissima Trinidad, Nelson's old acquaintance, as he used to call her, was distinguishable only by her four decks; and to the bow of his opponent he ordered the Victory to be steered. It is worthy of remark that he gained the highest honour in grappling with this ship in the action of Cape St. Vincent. She was the largest vessel in the world, and carried 136 guns.

The Victory had not yet returned a single gun, though fifty of her men had been killed or wounded. Nelson declared that in all his battles, he had seen nothing which surpassed the cool courage of his crew on this occasion. At four minutes after twelve, she opened her fire from both sides of her deck. For four hours, the conflict which ensued was tremendous. The Victory ran on board the Redoubtable, and was received with a broadside. The French ship then instantly let down her lower deck ports, for fear of being boarded through them, and never afterwards fired a great gun during the action. But her tops, like those of all the enemy's ships, were filled with riflemen, a practice Nelson never would adopt, not merely because it endangers setting fire to the sails, but because it is a murderous sort of warfare, by which individuals may suffer and a commander now and then be picked off, but which never can decide the fate of a general engagement. An incessant fire was kept up from the Victory from both sides, her larboard guns playing upon the Bucentaure and the huge Santissima Trinidad.

It had been part of a prayer composed by Nelson, just before going into action, that the British fleet might be distinguished by humanity in the victory which he expected. Setting an example himself, he twice gave orders to cease firing upon the Redoubtable, supposing that she had struck, because her great guns were silent; for, as she carried no flag, there were no means of instantly ascertaining the fact. From this ship, which he had thus twice spared, he received his death! A ball from her mizen-top, struck the epaulette on his left shoulder, about a quarter after one, just in the heat of the action. He fell upon his face, on the spot which was covered with the blood of his secretary Mr. Scott, who had fallen in the beginning of the action. Captain Hardy, who was a few steps from him, turning round saw three men raising him up. " They have done for me at last, Hardy!" said he; " I hope not," cried Hardy; " Yes," he replied, " my back-bone is shot through." The ball had passed through the spine, and lodged in the muscles of the back, towards the right side.

Even in this trying moment, Nelson did not lose his presence of mind. As the men were carrying him down the ladder, he observed that the tiller ropes which had been shot away were not yet replaced. He ordered new ones to be rove immediately; and then, that he might not be seen by the crew, he took out his handkerchief, and covered his face and his stars. It was soon perceived, upon examination, that his wound was mortal. He was in great pain, and expressed much anxiety for the event of the action which now began to declare itself. As often as a ship struck, the crew of the Victory hurraed; and at every hurra, a visible expression of joy gleamed in the eyes, and marked the countenance of the dying hero.

It was above an hour before Capt. Hardy could leave the deck, to attend the pallet of his expiring friend. At length he came. They shook hands in silence. " Well, Hardy," said Nelson, " how goes the day with us ?" —" Very well," replied Hardy; " ten ships have struck, but five of the van have tacked, and shew an intention to bear down upon the Victory. I have called two or three of our fresh ships round, and have no doubt of giving them a drubbing." " I hope," said Nelson, " none of our ships have struck." " There was no fear of that," answered Hardy. Then, and not till then, Nelson spoke of himself. " I am a dead man, Hardy," said he; " I am going fast. It will be all over with me soon." Hardy observed that he hoped Mr. Beatty (the surgeon) could yet hold out some prospect of life. " Oh no," he replied, " it is impossible. My back is shot through. Beatty will tell you so." Capt. Hardy then once more shook hands with him, and with a heart almost bursting hastened upon deck.

In about an hour he returned to the cockpit, and again taking the hand of his dying friend and commander, congratulated him on having gained a complete victory. How many of the enemy were taken he did not know, as it was impossible to perceive them distinctly; but fourteen or fifteen at least. " That's well," cried Nelson; " but I bargained for twenty; and then, in a stronger voice, he said; " Anchor, Hardy, anchor." Presently, calling him back, he said to him in a low tone, " don't throw me overboard ;" and he desired that he might be buried by his parents, unless it should please the King to order otherwise. He then reverted to private feelings, and said, " Kiss me, Hardy."—Hardy knelt down and kissed his cheek; and Nelson said, " Now I am satisfied : Thank God, I have done my duty." Hardy stood over him in silence for a moment or two; then knelt again, and kissed his forehead. " Who is that ?" said Nelson; and being informed, he replied, " God bless you Hardy !" And Hardy then left him—for ever !

Nelson now desired to be turned upon his right side, and said; " I wish I had not left the deck, for I shall soon be gone." Death was indeed rapidly approaching. He said to the chaplain, " Doctor, I have *not been a great* sinner." His articulation now became difficult; but he was distinctly heard to say, " Thank God ! I have done my duty!" These words he repeatedly pronounced, and they were the last which he uttered. He expired at thirty minutes after four—three hours and a quarter after he had received his wound. He was in the 47th year of his age. Once, amid his sufferings, he had expressed a wish that he were dead; but immediately the spirit subdued the pains of death, and he wished to live a little longer; doubtless, that he might hear the completion of the victory which he had seen so gloriously begun. That consolation, that joy, that triumph, was afforded him. He lived to know that the victory was decisive; and the last guns which were fired at the flying enemy, were heard a minute or two before he expired.

The total British loss in the battle of Trafalgar amounted to 1,587. Twenty of the enemy struck. Unhappily the fleet did not anchor, as Nelson almost with his dying breath had enjoined : a gale came on from the south west; some of the prizes went down; some went on shore ; one effected its escape into Cadiz; others were destroyed; four only were saved, and those by the greatest exertions. The Spanish Vice-Admiral Alva died of his wounds. Villeneuve was sent to England, and permitted to return to France.

" It is almost superfluous to add," observes his biographer, " that all the honours which a grateful nation could bestow were heaped upon the memory of Nelson. His brother was made an earl with a grant of £.6000 a year. £.10,000 were voted to each of his sisters, and £ 100,000 for the purchase of an estate. Statues and monuments were voted by most of our principal cities."   His body was brought home for interment.   It was exhibited for several days in the proudest state at Greenwich : from thence it was conveyed to Westminster, and finally buried at the public cost, in St. Paul's Cathedral, January 8th, 1806.

DESCRIPTION OF THE MEDAL.

OBVERSE.—Bust of his lordship by Webbe. The Inscription, " ADMIRAL LORD NELSON, K. B. DUKE OF BRONTE."

REVERSE.—A female standing on an antique galley ; the Lion's head on the prow of which designates her to be Britannia hurling thunder on her enemies. The inscription " NILE, 1ST OF AUGUST, 1798 ;—COPENHAGEN, 2ND APRIL, 1801 ;—TRAFALGAR, 21ST OCTOBER, 1805." points out the most memorable of the many victories in which he was engaged, and the whole forcibly illustrates the lines of Walter Scott,

> " To him, as to the burning leven,
> Short, bright, resistless course was given;
> Where'er his Country's foes were found,
> Was heard the fated thunders sound
> Till burst the bolt on yonder shore,
> Roll'd, blaz'd, destroy'd—and was no more."

No. VII.

ADMIRAL SIR SIDNEY SMITH.

WILLIAM SIDNEY SMITH was born in the year 1764, in the parish of St. Anne's, Soho, Westminster. He was the eldest son of Captain Smith, who accompanied Lord Sackville as his aid-de-camp in the war of 1756, and who afterwards obtained a place in the royal household. He acquired the rudiments of an excellent education at Tunbridge school, under the superintendance of Dr. Knox; and in 1777 he commenced his naval career. It is a curious circumstance, that the grandfather of Sir Sidney Smith, in his will, made a solemn request to his descendants, that " while a musquet or a ship remained to the country, his children would never embark in trade."

Shortly after his entering into the navy, he was placed in the Sandwich, under the command of Captain Young. He was rapidly promoted. From the Alcide of 74 guns, in which he was raised, in the year 1780, to the rank of fifth lieutenant, he was advanced to that of commander of the Fury, a sloop of 18 guns, on the Jamaica station. On the 7th of May 1783 he was made a post-captain, by commission, and appointed to the Nemesis, a frigate of 28 guns.

When the peace took place, his ardent and enterprising character could not adapt itself to the consequent inactivity; and about the year 1788 he solicited and obtained permission to enter into the Swedish service, where he greatly distinguished himself in the war which took place between that country and Russia. The King of Sweden bestowed upon him the Grand Cross of the Swedish Order of the Sword; and, in a letter written to his late majesty George III. accompanying the honourable insignia, Gustavus thus expressed himself:—" We have returned your Majesty what we had borrowed for our use during the late war, and what, had it been less valuable, we should have endeavoured to have retained. Captain Smith is an officer whom we shall long remember with gratitude."

After this Sir Sidney was for a short time employed in the Turkish

G

service, till he was recalled home by his Majesty's proclamation at the breaking out of the revolutionary war with France.

He hastened from Smyrna, and joined the fleet under Lord Hood, just before the conclusion of the siege of Toulon. This was a service peculiarly calculated for the display of his extraordinary powers. He harassed the vessels and craft of the enemy by incessant attacks, which were conceived with judgment and executed with vigour. Following their squadrons into their own ports, he at last forced an entry into the bay of Herqui (March 18, 1796), destroyed the batteries of its promontory, and burned the ships in the harbour. He at this time commanded the Diamond of 38 guns, to which he had been appointed in 1794.

The ardour and intrepidity of his conduct placed him, at last, a captive in the hands of the enemy. This disaster occurred on the 18th of April 1796. He was then stationed off Havre de Grace, where he observed one of the French lugger privateers which had been driven, by the strong setting-in of the tide, into the harbour, above the forts. He captured the privateer, but was compelled to remain in the same situation himself during the night. In the morning, the French discovered their lugger in the tow of a string of English boats. A signal of alarm was immediately given, and several gun-boats, and other armed vessels, bore down upon the English. All resistance soon became unavailing, and Sir Sidney, with not above nineteen of his gallant associates, were compelled to surrender themselves prisoners of war. He was conveyed to Paris, and sent, first, to the Abbaye, whence he was afterwards removed to the Temple. Here he was treated with great rigour, and every precaution was adopted that could prevent, as it was thought, the possibility of escape. Means, however, were found to baffle the vigilance of his gaolers, and by the aid of a fabricated order for his removal to another prison, he contrived to make his escape, and arrived in London in May 1798. He was welcomed in England by the general congratulations of the people, who considered his return as little less than a miracle.

In the month of June following Sir Sidney was appointed to the command of the Tiger of 80 guns, and in November he sailed for the Mediterranean, where he was honoured with a distinct command as an established commodore on the coast of Egypt. It was while he acted upon this station that he performed the brilliant achievement which has made his name so justly celebrated.

Buonaparte, who commanded the French army in Egypt, having determined to march against Acre, he crossed the little river of that name on the 18th of March 1799, and encamped upon an insulated eminence that was near to, and parallel with, the sea. On the 20th the trenches were opened, at about one hundred and fifty fathoms from the fortress. Ghezzar Bashaw, who commanded this place, sent timely notice to Sir Sidney Smith of the intended advance of Buonaparte, and on the 7th of March he sailed for the coast of Syria. On the 11th he arrived before Carissa, and on the fifteenth steered for St. John D'Acre, to concert measures with Ghezzar, having got the start of the enemy by two days, which he employed in making preparations for defence. He had captured, in his passage, the whole French flotilla, under the command of Eydoun, laden with heavy cannon, ammunition, platforms, and other articles necessary for Buonaparte's army to undertake the siege. This artillery, consisting of 44 pieces, was immediately mounted on the ramparts of Acre against the lines and batteries of the enemy, as well as on gun vessels.

On the 30th of March the French effected a breach in the wall on the north-east part of the town, and endeavoured to take it by assault, but were vigorously repulsed by the garrison with considerable loss. The ditch was filled with dead bodies. The troops of Ghezzar afterwards made three successful sorties, in the last of which the English destroyed the whole construction of a mine which had been prepared by the enemy. It was judged, indeed, to be the best mode of defence, by the garrison, to make frequent sorties, in order to keep the French on the defensive, and to impede the progress of their covering works.

On the 28th of April, the French were encouraged by the arrival of three pieces of battering artillery, 24 pounders, and six pieces of eighteen. The English also received reinforcements, by the timely arrival, on the 7th of May, in the bay of Acre, of a fleet of corvettes and transports under the command of Hassin Bey.

The approach of this additional strength was the signal to Buonaparte for a most vigorous and persevering assault, in the hope of getting possession of the town before the reinforcements could disembark. The gun-boats, which were within grape distance of the head of the attacking column, added to the Turkish musquetry, did great execution ; but still the enemy gained ground. They had made a lodgment on the second story of the north-east tower, the upper part being entirely battered down, and the ruins of the ditch forming the ascent by which they mounted. On the morning of the 8th of May the French standard floated on the outer angle of the tower. Hassan Bey's troops were in the boats, but as yet only half way on the shore. This was a most critical part of the contest; and an effort was necessary to preserve the place for a short time, till their arrival. Sir Sidney, therefore, landed the boats at the Mole, and took the crews, armed with pikes, up to the breach. The enthusiastic gratitude of the Turks, men, women, and children, at the sight of such a reinforcement at such a time can hardly be described. A fierce and sanguinary conflict now took place, which continued the whole of the day, and during which Sir Sidney displayed the most heroic courage, as well as the most consummate talents in conducting the defence of the place. A little before sunset, a massive column of the enemy appeared advancing to the breach with a solemn step. The Bashaw's idea was, not to defend the breach this time, but rather to let a certain number of the enemy in, and then close with them, according to the Turkish mode of warfare. The French column consequently mounted the breach unmolested, and descended from the rampart into the Bashaw's garden, where, in a very few moments, the bravest and most advanced among them lay headless corpses : the sabre, with the addition of the dagger in the other hand, proving more than a match for the bayonet. The rest retreated precipitately.

The next night, the 9th of May, the Turkish Chifflick regiment made itself master of the enemy's third parallel, by an intrepid sortie. A flag of truce was now sent into the town by the hand of an Arabian dervise, with a letter to the Bashaw, proposing a cessation of arms, for the purpose of burying the dead bodies, the stench from which had become intolerable, and threatened the existence of both armies, many having died delirious a few hours after being seized with the first symptoms of infection. While the answer was under consideration, a volley of shot and shells, on a sudden, announced an assault, which, however, the garrison was ready to receive, and the assailants only contributed to increase the dead bodies, " to the eternal disgrace," observed Sir Sidney in his dispatch, " of the general who thus disloyally sacrificed them."

All hopes of success being now utterly at an end, the enemy had no alternative but to retreat, which he accordingly did, in the night, between the 20th and 21st of May, after a siege of sixty days! This was the first check which Buonaparte received, in his military career, from the skill and bravery of a British general and British troops. How little did he then dream that from the same source was to flow the tide that finally overwhelmed him!

Description of the Medal.

Obverse.—Bust of Sir Sidney in his naval uniform.

Reverse.—The memorable and most important defence of St. Jean D'Acre by this officer is represented by a Lion protecting a defenceless Camel (the symbolical representative of Syria) from the attacks of a Tiger (France).—Inscription— " Acre defended—Buonaparte repulsed—Syria saved—20th May, 1799."

No. VIII.

SIR RALPH ABERCROMBY.

THIS distinguished and lamented officer was the son of George Abercromby, Esq. of Tillibodie in Clackmannanshire. The date of his birth is uncertain. According to some accounts he was born about the year 1738; but the inscription on the monument erected to his memory at Malta, places that event in 1733. Having received a liberal education, he chose the army for his profession, and received his first commission as a cornet in the 3rd regiment of dragoon guards on the 23d March 1756. In the month of February 1760, he obtained a lieutenancy in the same regiment, and in the following April a company in the third regiment of horse. In this last corps he rose to the rank of major and lieutenant-colonel. In November 1780 he was included in a list of brevet colonels, and in 1781 was made colonel of the 103d, or King's Irish infantry. In 1787 (September 26th) he was promoted to the rank of major-general.

When the French revolutionary war broke out, he was employed on the Continent, and had the local rank of lieutenant-general conferred upon him. On every occasion his bravery and skill procured him the warmest praise of the commander in chief, and of the army. He led the advanced guard in the action on the heights at Cateau, and was wounded at Nimeguen. In the disastrous retreat from Holland in the winter of 1794, he eminently distinguished himself. In 1795 he was made Knight of the Bath, and appointed commander in chief of the forces in the West Indies. During his abode on this station he made several important conquests (Grenada, Trinidad, and the settlements of Demerara and Essequibo among others), and after a most successful campaign returned to England 1797, when he received the command of the 2d or North British Dragoons. He had previously been raised to the rank of lieutenant-general; and he was now made governor of the Isle of Wight, from which, however, he was removed in 1798, and appointed to the higher office of governor of Fort St. George, and Fort Augustus.

During the early part of the rebellion in Ireland, he filled the station of commander in chief in that country, and displayed the most amiable union of firmness and humanity in the execution of that delicate trust. His name is still revered by those who witnessed his benevolent conduct, and participated in its consequences. When it was found necessary to blend the civil and military command in the same person (the Marquis of Cornwallis), General Abercromby was removed to the chief command in Scotland.

In the expedition against Holland, Sir Ralph Abercromby held a principal command under His Royal Highness the Duke of York, and the talents, activity, and bravery which he displayed, added fresh honours to his name.

At length the moment arrived when he was to inscribe his fame in the imperishable annals of his country. In 1801, the memorable expedition to Egypt was undertaken, in order to drive the French from that country. To Sir Ralph Abercromby was entrusted the command of that expedition, and on the 8th of March 1801, he landed the English army at Aboukir, in the face of the enemy, who kept up a most destructive fire upon the boats as they approached the shore. Nothing, however, could dismay our troops. Through a fire, rendered doubly tremendous by the impossibility of resistance, they continued steadily to advance, cheering and huzzaing as if victory had already been within their grasp. Numbers were destroyed in this gallant enterprise. Some were shot in the boats, and others bayoneted as they stepped out of them, by the enemy, who had come down to the water's edge to receive them as they landed. The British, however, formed immediately after they quitted the boats, and lost not a moment in advancing.

The contest on the shore lasted about twenty minutes, when the enemy gave way in every quarter, and our brave fellows remained completely victorious. During the following days the rest of the army, together with the baggage, provisions, and stores of all kinds, were safely landed, the French not daring to shew themselves, or to attempt any kind of hostility against us.

On the morning of the 12th March, the army moved from their position in two columns, and continued to advance without meeting any serious opposition, till they arrived upon the ground where it was determined to give battle. Sir Ralph formed the troops into two lines which extended from the sea to lake Mareotis and lake Aboukir. The French were drawn up in our front, occupying a very strong position along a range of hills. It was determined to attempt driving the enemy from this position, and orders were given for marching forward at day-break on the 13th. From some untoward circumstances, however, it was half past six, instead of five, before the army began to move. As they advanced, the French commenced a destructive fire upon them from a numerous and admirably well served flying artillery, which caused great havoc. The battle soon became general along the whole line of both armies, and continued till half past eleven, when the French, hard pressed by our steady fire, began to retreat from hill to hill till they were close under the walls of Alexandria. Here they rallied upon the heights, and Sir Ralph Abercromby, perceiving that if he were to dislodge the enemy, he could not himself retain possession of those heights, as they were commanded by two forts, he determined not to make the attempt. Our loss in this victory was considerable.

The two armies remained in sight of each other during the six subsequent days, and were actively engaged in fortifying their respective positions. On the 21st March, at half past three in the morning, just as our troops were getting under arms, they were alarmed by a pretty smart fire of musquetry, proceeding from the canal towards their left. This was supposed to be merely a feint, to harass the men, or try their alertness, for Sir Ralph Abercromby was not aware of the junction of all the French forces at Alexandria. The object of the enemy in making this attack, as it afterwards appeared, was to turn and overthrow the reserve, which was separated a little from the rest of the army. This accomplished, their next aim was to force our centre with their united troops, and while the attention of the left was fully occupied by the false attack, the whole force of their cavalry, in which they were very strong, was to avail itself of a favourable opportunity, and, by an impetuous charge, decide the contest. Repulsed, however, in every quarter, and finding it impossible to penetrate through any part of our line, the French infantry at length gave way, and dispersed in all directions. General Menou then determined to make a last desperate effort at carrying our position. He ordered the main body of the cavalry to charge, supported by the brigades in reserve. Accordingly a furious onset was made, and the enemy charged through the 42nd regiment, reaching as far as their tents. Here, however, they were effectually stopped; the horses, entangled in the cords, were for the most part killed; while many of the men were obliged to seek their safety on foot. At this juncture, the Minorca regiment came to the support of the 42nd, when a second time the French cavalry advanced, and made another desperate charge upon those regiments. As it would have been impossible to withstand the shock, they opened with the most deliberate composure to let them pass; then, facing about, they poured upon them such volleys as brought numbers both of men and horses to the ground. The cavalry now endeavoured to force its way back, but this they were unable to effect, and the greater part were either killed or wounded in the attempt. A standard was taken, covered with the military exploits of the corps to which it belonged.

It must have been at this period that the gallant veteran, Sir R. Abercromby, received his mortal wound. It was impossible to ascertain the exact moment, for he never complained, or revealed the circumstance, till it was perceived by those about him. No intreaty, even then, could induce him to leave the field, before he was convinced, by his own observation, of the retreat of the enemy. When he beheld this gratifying sight, which was about half past nine, he attempted to get on horseback, but his wound, which had been probed, and dressed in the field, having become extremely stiff and painful, he could not mount. He, therefore, suffered himself, though very reluctantly, to be placed upon a litter, from which he was removed into a boat, and carried on board the Foudroyant, where Lord Keith received him with all possible kindness. The ball had entered the thigh very high up, and taking a direction towards the groin had lodged in the bone, whence it could not be extracted. A fever ensued, and mortification taking place, his death was inevitable. That lamented event took place on the night of the 28th, seven days after the battle. During the whole of that time the anguish and torture he endured were extreme. Yet, not a groan, not a complaint, escaped his lips.

In the action on the 13th of March, he had suffered a contusion in the

H

thigh from a musquet ball, and had a horse killed under him. On the 21st, at the time he received his death wound, he was in the very midst of the enemy, and personally engaged with a French officer of dragoons, who was at that moment shot by a corporal of the 42nd. Sir Ralph retained the officer's sword which had passed between his arm and his side the instant before he fell.

His remains were conveyed to Malta, where they were interred in the Castle of St. Elmo in La Valetta, on the 29th of April. A suitable epitaph, written in latin, by the Abbé Navarrio, librarian to the order of Malta, is inscribed on a slab of black marble over the grave where he reposes. As a testimony of national regard, however, the House of Commons voted a monument to his memory in St. Paul's cathedral, and a pension of £.2,000 was settled on his family. His widow was created Baroness Abercromby, with remainder to her issue male by her late husband.

DESCRIPTION OF THE MEDAL.

OBVERSE.—Bust of Lieutenant General Sir Ralph Abercromby.

REVERSE.—The horse starting as he advances, and the three pyramids behind, plainly refer to a transaction in Egypt, which the inscription round the face of the reverse, and the date of the exergue, shew to be the hostile reception experienced by the British on their landing in Egypt for the purpose of expelling the French from that country. Both the obverse and the reverse are of masterly execution. The horse is of that noble species, of that high mettle, which is alone worthy of typifying the character of the brave army which performed those exploits in Egypt which must ever live in military renown. He receives a momentary impression, but is so far from retreating, that he makes good his stand. The bust is an extraordinary specimen of medallic engraving of nearly a front view. Its drawing, its likeness, its fleshiness and neatness, place the English artist (Webb) among the very first of modern Medallists in the class of busts.

No. IX.

EGYPT DELIVERED.

JOHN HELY HUTCHINSON, Lord Hutchinson, Baron of Alexandria, was born on the 15th May 1757. He is the second son of Christiana, baroness of Donoughmore, by the late Right Hon. John Hely Hutchinson, principal Secretary of State for Ireland, and keeper of His Majesty's signet or privy seal. This gentleman was a conspicuous political character in Ireland, during the latter half of the last century.

Lord Hutchinson, who is next brother to the present Earl of Donoughmore, was educated at Eton College, and the University of Dublin. He entered very early in life into the military service of his country, and as he devoted himself with much ardour to its duties, his promotion, aided by the influence of his family, was consequently rapid.

When the British army, under the lamented Sir Ralph Abercromby was sent to the shores of Egypt, he was appointed second in command, and upon the death of Sir Ralph, in the memorable battle of Aboukir, the chief command of the troops necessarily devolved upon him. It was on this occasion that he displayed those great military talents, whose successful exertion obtained for him a title. Under his authority the capitulation of Cairo took place on the 17th June 1801, which was followed by the surrender of Alexandria, and the final evacuation of Egypt by the French. In reward for these distinguished services, General Hutchinson was advanced to the dignity of a British peerage, and on the 16th of December 1801, received the unanimous thanks of both Houses of Parliament, and a pension of £.2,000 per annum.

The capitulation by which Egypt was entirely freed from the presence of the French armies, was signed on the 31st of August 1801. General Menou found it impossible to maintain himself in Alexandria any longer, against the combined land and sea forces of the British, by which that city was blockaded; and on the 30th of August at two o'clock in the afternoon one of his aid-de-camps arrived at General Hutchinson's head quarters with the proposed terms of surrender. Some of these terms, however, were so ridiculous and absurd, that they were peremptorily rejected, and an answer returned that the armistice would be annulled, and hostilities immediately recommenced if Menou did not consider better of his demands. Amended articles of capitulation were then proposed on the 31st, and being acceded to with some explanatory additions on the part of General Hutchinson, the British army took possession of the French lines at 12 o'clock on the 2nd of September. The victorious troops marched in with all the bands playing and drums beating, and the British and Turkish flags were immediately hoisted together. Thus was a glorious campaign terminated, by giving us the entire possession of Egypt, and an enemy, who during the war had considered himself invincible, was taught that British troops meeting him on fair ground, knew how to maintain their ancient superiority.

DESCRIPTION OF THE MEDAL.

OBVERSE. — A three-quarter bust of Lord Hutchinson, in his regimentals, by Webb.

REVERSE. — General Hutchinson and the Bey of Egypt concluding their final treaty, previously to the departure of the British force which had expelled the French from that country.

Pl. 3.

IX

X

XI

XII

London, Pub. July 1st 1820, by Henry Colburn & Co Conduit Street.

No. X.

A SCOTTISH SOLDIER.

THE late war shed one common blaze of glory upon the arms of the United Kingdoms, and it would be impossible, even if it were desirable, to separate the respective shares which each country contributed towards the production of that glory. England, Ireland, and Scotland—the sons of the Thames, the Tweed, and the Shannon, stood gallantly forth to assert the liberties of mankind, and approving Heaven smiled upon their cause. If there was rivalry among them, it was the noble rivalry of which should be foremost in the discharge of a general duty: if there was pre-eminence, it was won from opportunity alone. No individual, no regiment of England, achieved deeds which would not have been equally achieved by an individual, or a regiment of Scotland and Ireland. The same may be predicated alternately of each country.

With respect to the national valour, which is commemorated by this medal, its exploits will grace many a fair page in the future history of the country. Upon the arid plains of Egypt, in the mountainous passes of Spain and Portugal, on the soil of France, and in the bloody field of Waterloo, Scottish heroism won imperishable fame. We cannot, however, better describe its martial qualities, than in the glowing language of Scotia's own inspired bard.

" But bring a Scotsman frae his hill,
Clap in his cheek a Highland gill,
Say, such is royal George's will,
    An there's the foe,
He has nae thought but how to kill
    Twa at a blow.
" Nae cauld, faint-hearted doubtings tease him,
Death comes—wi' fearless eye he sees him ;

Wi' bluidy hand a welcome gies him,
          An when he fa's,
His latest draught o' breathin lea'es him
          In faint huzzas."

                                                                                BURNS.

DESCRIPTION OF THE MEDAL.

OBVERSE. — The bust of a Scottish Soldier, in his military accoutrements, with the motto, " *Nemo me impune lacessit.*"   The meaning and spirit of this motto has been felt and understood by the enemy in the late campaigns.   It is properly coupled with the national emblem of the thistle, on the reverse of this medal.

REVERSE. — United branches of the laurel and thistle, with the dates and names occupying the middle of the Medal, and shewing the different countries in which Scottish valour had signalised itself within the two stated periods.

No. XI.

FOUNDATION OF THE ROYAL MILITARY COLLEGE.

THE services which the illustrious individual whose bust is on the obverse of this medal, has rendered to the British army, during the long series of years in which he has presided over its interests, and regulated its general discipline and management, are the theme of eulogy with every one whom professional knowledge qualifies to judge upon such a subject. To his unabated exertions it is owing that the British army at this moment offers a model of perfection to every military nation. On various occasions, when discussions have arisen in Parliament connected with the army, the most unequivocal testimony has been borne to the distinguished merits of His Royal Highness. They, indeed, who remember what was the system pursued thirty years ago, and compare it with the one now in operation, must acknowledge that in no public department of the state have such signal improvements been introduced. Even during the period when His Royal Highness was persecuted by a despicable faction, who succeeded in raising a popular prejudice against him for a time, calumny itself could not deny that he was the ablest commander in chief this country ever possessed.

His impartial dispensation of promotion, and his anxious desire to reward the services of the meritorious officer, are acknowledged not only by the whole army, but by the country at large. That private feelings, whether of attachment or prejudice, may sometimes influence his decisions, is only to say, in other words, that he is man, and susceptible of human passions ; but that he has ever allowed such feelings to acquire an undue ascendancy, or permitted his sense of duty to be palpably biassed by them, is disproved by the affection which the whole army bears towards him. The soldier regards him as his father; the subaltern officer as his patron ; and the meritorious of all ranks, as their friend.

In discharging the multifarious duties of his office he is indefatigable, and the hours which he devotes to their laborious discharge, would be deemed a hardship by the youngest clerk at the Horse Guards. Every arrangement, the most minute, is submitted by the heads of departments for his sanction. The memorial of every officer, the petition of every soldier, engages his perusal or attention, nor are any suffered to pass unnoticed.

It would be injustice not to mention, that when the general peace was concluded in 1814, and our gallant soldiers returned to their native country, full of honours and renown, the House of Commons came to a deliberate vote of thanks to his Royal Highness, for the signal ability he had manifested in discharging the functions of his office. This vote is thus recorded in the journals of the House of Commons:

" 6th July 1814. Resolved, that the Speaker do signify by letter to the Duke of York the thanks voted to the army, and that in addressing his Royal Highness he do particularly express the high sense which the House entertains of his Royal Highness's long, unremitting, and effectual exertions for the improvement of the British army."

In addition to this solemn recognition of his Royal Highness's merits, it may be mentioned that the Duke of Wellington, when he received, in person, the thanks of both Houses of Parliament for his great services to Europe, ascribed no small part of the victories he had gained, to the high and efficient state of discipline of the troops which were sent out to him. It is no exaggerated eulogy, therefore, to say, that whenever that event shall happen, which will necessarily remove his Royal Highness from the post he now occupies, to fill the most august station in the empire, the change will prove a serious loss to the British army.

The noble institution, commemorated on the reverse of the present medal, is one of the many proofs which his Royal Highness has given, of his provident anxiety for the permanent good of the army. It was solely from his recommendation, and from the strong grounds of expediency which he laid before his late Majesty, that the Royal Military College at Sandhurst was established.

This College consists of two separate departments, called the *Senior* and the *Junior*. The former was founded in 1799, and the latter in 1802. Each department has its specific object.

The senior department was established for the purpose of instructing officers in the scientific parts of their duty, with a view to enable them more efficiently to discharge that duty when acting in the command of regiments.

The junior department is for the instruction of those who from early life are intended for the military profession. With this purpose is combined also, one of benevolence, for it is made to afford a provision for the sons of meritorious officers who have fallen, or have been disabled, in the service of their country, and the means of educating the sons of officers belonging to the regular service.

The national importance of such an establishment has been acknowledged by every one qualified to appreciate its value. Heretofore, it had been unwisely thought that every thing might be learned in the field; that practice was the best school; and that theoretical generals were not very often the most efficient commanders in the day of battle. Mere speculative knowledge, indeed, will qualify no man for any course of life : but it should be remembered, that the great leading characters of practice are mostly reducible to certain axioms. The art of war, like every other art, is founded upon fixed principles, and without the knowledge of these no certain results can be calculated upon. It was surely an improvident system, therefore, which left the youthful soldier no other school but actual service, and which abandoned him to the necessity of acquiring experience too often through the medium of defeat and disgrace. This dangerous anomaly, however, is no longer our reproach. The military College at Sandhurst, and other establishments which have been either wholly organized or greatly improved by his Royal Highness the commander-in-chief, provide, at least, the means of acquiring the elements of military tactics.

Her late Majesty presented the colours (the ceremony of which is commemorated on the reverse of this medal) to the gentlemen cadets on the 12th of August 1813, as a token of the interest which she felt for the prosperity of the institution.

DESCRIPTION OF THE MEDAL.

OBVERSE.—Head of the Duke, with the inscription round the face of the Medal—" FIELD MARSHAL F. DUKE OF YORK."

I

REVERSE.—The Queen presenting Colours to the Students of the Military College, at Sandhurst. On one of the Colours is the motto—" VIRES ACQUIRIT EUNDO." Behind are the College portico, and two attendants on her Majesty, one of them the Duke of York, the founder of the College. Above is this legend—" PRESENTATION OF COLOURS BY HER MAJESTY, AUGUST, 1813." On the exergue is the College, with the date of its foundation.

The head of the Duke has a beautiful firmness, delicacy of outline, and texture of flesh and hair. The execution is highly honourable to the English Artist, Mr. Webb. The figures on the reverse are marked with great neatness and precision. The design on this reverse is peculiarly appropriate to the general subject of the Medals, as this College is very justly acknowledged to be one of the best nurseries of that military excellence which has conducted the British arms to its present zenith of glory, under the able superintendance of the commander-in-chief.

ARRIVAL OF THE ENGLISH ARMY IN THE PENINSULA.

THE illustrious General, who forms the subject of this Medal, was born May 1, 1769, being the fifth son of the late Earl of Mornington. The family from which he is descended (that of Cowley or Colley) was of English origin, and settled in the county of Rutland. In the reign of Henry VIII. it migrated to Ireland, and that country has to boast of having given birth to the greatest warrior of modern times. The seat of his ancestors (Dengan Castle) was the place of his nativity, but, when he attained a sufficient age, he was sent to Eton. An early and decided predilection for a military life occasioned his removal from that celebrated seminary before he had time to acquire those scholastic advantages which a longer abode there would have secured. From Eton he went to Angers in France, and in the military academy of that town he prosecuted studies which were congenial to his nature. On the 25th December 1787, being then in his eighteenth year, Mr. Wellesley received an ensign's commission in the 41st regiment.

England was then enjoying a profound peace, and Ensign Wellesley had no immediate prospect of gratifying his wishes by signalizing himself in active service. Meanwhile, however, he continued to rise in rank. On the 23d January 1788 he obtained a lieutenancy; and on the 30th June 1791 he was appointed Captain in the 58th or Rutlandshire regiment. On the 30th April 1793 he received a majority in the 33d regiment; and on the 30th September, in the same year, he purchased a lieutenant-colonelcy in it.

The year 1794 may be regarded as the commencement of that career whose glorious progress and termination will form a bright page in the annals of England. Lieutenant-colonel Wellesley was with his regiment in the expedition under Lord Moira, which landed on the coast of Britanny. The troops composing this expedition were subsequently compelled to hasten to the relief of the Duke of York in the Netherlands, and

Lieutenant-colonel Wellesley, at the head of three battalions, covered all the movements of the army during the disastrous retreat that followed. It is said that on this occasion he displayed a degree of coolness and skill which excited the highest admiration among those officers who witnessed his conduct.

In 1797 the Earl of Mornington (now Marquis Wellesley) was nominated Governor General of India, and his brother, Colonel Wellesley, went out to that country with his regiment (the 33d) in the same year. We cannot enter into the details of his military achievements in the East, which could have been surpassed only by his own more renowned exploits afterwards in Europe. At the memorable siege of Seringapatam he signally distinguished himself as far as any opportunity for doing so was afforded him; and he was subsequently appointed to the command of that city, when it passed, with the other dominions of Tippoo, into our possession. " The command of Seringapatam," observed Lord Mornington, in one of his dispatches to the Court of Directors, " will remain in the hands of Colonel Wellesley. It is a trust of great delicacy and importance, which it is my duty to repose in a person of approved military talents and integrity." On the 25th July 1801 he was gazetted as brigadier-general of the English army in Egypt, though, in point of fact, he never joined the troops under the command of Sir Ralph Abercromby.

It was in India that this great commander gained his first victory, and displayed those consummate talents in the field which afterwards raised him to so proud a height of glory. The battle of Assye, which was fought on the 24th Sept. 1802, exhibited all those peculiar features which, expanded upon a wider theatre, and dignified by a mightier stake, have filled Europe with his renown. It was distinguished by three circumstances, all of them component parts of his subsequent achievements, viz. the promptitude with which he changed his proposed mode of attack, even though in actual march to execute it; his determination to engage with an inferior force, rather than by waiting for his own troops to arrive, also give time for the enemy to receive reinforcements; and lastly, the ready abandonment of his cannon, when he found that the difficulty of advancing it checked the more valuable rapidity of his movements. This victory was no less decisive in its consequences, than brilliant in its character, for it led to the pacification of India. The thanks of both Houses of Parliament were bestowed upon him, May 3, 1804, and he was elected a Knight Companion of the most honourable Order of the Bath.

In March 1805 he returned to England, and in 1806 took his seat in Parliament as Member for Newport in Hampshire. In the same year, on the 10th April, he was married to the present Duchess of Wellington. This lady was the Hon. Catherine Packenham, third daughter of Edward Lord Longford.

In 1807 Sir Arthur Wellesley was appointed Chief Secretary of Ireland, during the viceroyalty of the Duke of Richmond, and in the same year he accepted a command under Lord Cathcart in the expedition which was fitted out against Copenhagen. On this occasion also he eminently distinguished himself; and again received the thanks of the House of Commons as one of the officers who were employed on that memorable service.

The following year (1808) saw him land upon the coast of Portugal at the head of a small army which was intended merely to assist the Portuguese in throwing off the detestable yoke of France. How little did Napoleon, how little did Europe, how little did England herself think, at that moment, what a rich harvest of glory he was destined to reap. The rest of his biography is written in the annals of his country, and commemorated in our medallic series. The separate description which we have to give of his principal victories will form the noblest history of his life. From the lines of Torres Vedras he marched step by step, in the track of victory, dispersing the hostile legions that opposed him, baffling the skill of the ablest generals in Europe, and beating them by the superior energies of his comprehensive mind, not by the decisive superiority of numbers. He turned the arms of the oppressors on themselves. The invaders became the invaded : the conquerors were the conquered ; the imperial eagle, dabbled with blood, and checked in her towering flight, fled in terror before him. He entered the Peninsula, and saw it, in dreary prospect before him, bowed down in its captivity; he left it, and looking behind him from the lofty summit of its Pyrenean frontiers, beheld it smiling and grateful, freed from an odious bondage, standing erect again, and breathing the free air of liberty. " The military triumphs," to use the energetic language of the late Speaker of the House of Commons (now Lord Colchester), " which his valour achieved on the banks of the Douro and the Tagus, of the Ebro and the Garonne, called forth the spontaneous shouts of admiring nations." This eulogy was pronounced before the battle of Waterloo. In what terms of wonder and delight could the same accomplished orator have conveyed the feelings of England and of Europe at that stupendous triumph ?

Description of the Medal.

Obverse.—Head of the Duke, in imitation of the antique ; inscription, " arthur duke of wellington."

Reverse.—An allegorical display of the arrival of the British army in the Peninsula, to assist it against the French, whose military power and success in that country are pourtrayed by the eagle with the fulmen or thunder-bolt pursuing the armed force of Spain and Portugal, who are personated by two females imploring British aid. Round the face of the Medal is inscribed, " the english army arrives in the peninsula." On the exergue, or small division of the Medal, parted off from the subject, is the date of the arrival. In the back ground are the mountains peculiar to the country, which are also represented by the pillars of Hercules, the ancient emblems of the Peninsula.

Pl. 4.

XIII

XIV

XV

XVI

Normand fils.

London, Pub. July 1.st 1820, by Henry Colburn & C.o Conduit Street.

No. XIII.

THE BATTLE OF VIMIERA.

AS it is the object of the present work merely to supply such descriptive and historical details of particular events, as may serve to illustrate the medals which record them, we shall not blend with the account of the battle of Vimiera, any reflections upon the singular circumstances which accompanied and preceded it. The reader will understand that we allude to the successive appointments of different commanders in chief, in the persons of Sir Arthur Wellesley, Sir Harry Burrard, and Sir Hugh Dalrymple. Our business is with the first only.

The battle of Vimiera was fought on Sunday the 21st of August, 1808. Sir Arthur Wellesley, aware of the intention of the enemy to attack him, ordered all the troops to be under arms at sun rise. He had taken up a strong position, about a mile in front of the village of Vimiera, which is situated in a valley with the river Maceira running through it. To the westward and northward of this village, there is a mountain, the western point of which touches the sea, while the eastern is separated by a deep ravine, from the heights over which passes the road leading from Lourinha to Vimiera. On this mountain the greater part of the British army was placed, namely, the 1st, 2nd, 3rd, 4th, 5th, and 8th brigades with eight pieces of artillery, Major General Hill's brigade being on the right, and Major General Ferguson's on the left, having one battalion on the heights separated from the mountains. Brigadier General Fane was posted with his riflemen on a hill, as were also the 50th regiment, and Brigadier General Anstruther with his brigade, and half a brigade of six pounders. The cavalry and the reserve of artillery were in the valley between the hills on which the infantry stood, both flanking and supporting Brigadier General Fane's advanced guard.

The enemy commanded by General Junot in chief, and Generals Laborde and Loison, first appeared about eight o'clock in the morning, in large bodies of cavalry on our left, upon the heights on the road to Lourinha. It was apparent, therefore, that the attack was to be made on our advanced guard and the left of our position. To counteract this, Major General Ferguson's brigade was immediately ordered to move across the ravine, to the heights on the road to Lourinha, with three pieces of cannon. He was followed by the brigade of Major General Nightingale and three pieces of cannon; the brigade of Brigadier General Acland, and the brigade of Brigadier General Bowes. These troops were formed on those heights, with their right upon the valley which leads into Vimiera, and their left upon the other ravine, which separates those heights from the range that terminates at the landing place at Maceira. Major General Ferguson's brigade was in the first line; Brigadier General Nightingale's in the second; and Brigadier Generals Bowes' and Acland's in columns in the rear. The Portuguese troops, supported by Brigadier General Crawford's brigade, were posted, in the first instance, on the range which terminates, as above stated, at the landing place at Maceira. The troops of the advanced guard, on the height to the southward and eastward of the town, were deemed sufficient for its defence, and Major General Hill was moved to the centre of the mountain, on which the great body of the infantry had been posted, as a support to them. They also had, in addition, the support of the cavalry in the rear of their right.

The enemy advanced, confident of success. Their attack began in several columns upon the whole of the troops who were stationed on the heights above described. Such, indeed, was the ardor of their onset, that on the left they approached, in spite of the fire of the riflemen, close to the 50th regiment, and were driven back only by the well-applied bayonets of that intrepid corps. The second battalion of the 43d regiment was also closely engaged, in the road which leads into Vimiera, a part of that corps having been ordered into the churchyard to prevent them from reaching the town.

On the right of the position the enemy were also repulsed, by the bayonets of the 97th regiment, supported by the second battalion of the 52nd, which, advancing in column, took the French in flank. While the action was thus vigorously carried on between the enemy and the advanced guard, the former were attacked in flank by General Acland's brigade, as it advanced to its position on the heights. A brisk cannonade was also kept up on the flank of the enemy's columns by the artillery on those heights. At length, after a most desperate contest, they were driven back in confusion, with the loss of seven pieces of cannon, many prisoners, and a great number of officers and soldiers killed and wounded. They were vigorously pursued by the detachment of the 20th light dragoons; but their cavalry was so much superior in numbers, that this detachment suffered severely, and Lieutenant Colonel Taylor was unfortunately killed.

Nearly at the same time that this attack commenced upon the advanced guard, an engagement also took place on the road to Lourinha. The French rushed forward with their usual impetuosity, but they were received so steadily and coolly by Major General Ferguson's brigade, that their ardour was soon checked. This brigade consisted of the 36th, 46th, and 71st regiments, and as soon as the enemy approached they made a desperate charge upon them. They immediately gave way, while our troops continued to advance, supported by the 82nd (one of the corps of Brigadier General Nightingales' brigade), by the 29th, and by Brigadier General Bowes' and Acland's brigades. Meanwhile, Brigadier General Crawford's brigade, and the Portuguese troops in two lines, advanced along the heights on the left. In this action, six pieces of cannon were taken from the enemy, with many prisoners; and vast numbers were killed or wounded. They afterwards attempted to recover part of their artillery, by attacking the 71st and 82nd regiments, which were halted in a valley. In this enterprise, however, they were disappointed. Those regiments immediately retired from the low grounds to the heights, halted, faced about, fired, and then rushed upon the enemy, who had by that time arrived in the low grounds, and again compelled them to retire with great loss.

The battle was now decided, and victory declared for the British, who had fought under many disadvantages. The army of Sir Arthur Wellesley amounted to about 17,000 men, in conjunction with 1,600 Portuguese. But one half of this number was not engaged at all, while the enemy were decidedly superior in cavalry and artillery. Our loss was four officers, 131 men, killed; 37 officers, 497 men, wounded; two officers, 49 men, missing. The enemy lost nearly 4000, and 13 pieces of cannon. General Bernier was wounded and taken prisoner. The want of cavalry saved the

K

enemy from pursuit, or they would infallibly have sustained a still more signal defeat.

The result of this action was, that General Kellerman came in from the French lines, on the following day, with a flag of truce from Junot, to propose a cessation of hostilities, preparatory to concluding a convention for the evacuation of Portugal by the French troops. This convention was finally agreed upon, under the auspices of Sir Hugh Dalrymple who arrived at the British head quarters the day after the victory, to supersede Sir Harry Burrard, who, the day before the victory, had himself arrived to supersede Sir Arthur Wellesley! Finding, however, that Sir Arthur had made all the arrangements for giving battle to the enemy, he wisely abstained from any interference. " I was fortunate enough," he observed, in his dispatch to Lord Castlereagh, " to reach the field of action in time to witness and approve of every disposition that had been and was afterwards made by Sir Arthur Wellesley, his comprehensive mind furnishing a ready resource in every emergency, and rendering it quite unnecessary to direct any alteration."

The convention with Junot was signed on the 30th of August. It was the memorable *Convention of Cintra.* We need say no more. To discuss its merits, or to record the feelings it excited throughout the Country, comes not within the scope of this work. We conclude, therefore, with stating, that Portugal was evacuated by the French troops, and that the English entered Lisbon, on the 11th September, amid the joyful acclamations of the people. They had been sorely plundered and oppressed during the short dominion of their *liberators,* as the invading hordes of Napoleon styled themselves; and they were but too happy in escaping from their rapacious and insolent tyranny.

DESCRIPTION OF THE MEDAL.

OBVERSE.—The success of the Battle of Vimiera is pourtrayed by the triumphal car filled with military trophies, and conducted by the Goddess of Victory.

REVERSE.—The important consequence of the victory of Vimiera, was the occupation of Lisbon by the British, which city is here seen with the shipping on the Tagus.

No. XIV.

SIR JOHN MOORE.

SIR JOHN MOORE was born at Glasgow, November 13, 1761.
He was the son of Dr. Moore, the author of some popular productions
in his time, though few, if any, of them are likely to reach posterity.
In 1776 he obtained an ensigncy in the 51st regiment of foot, then
quartered at Minorca. He was afterwards promoted to a lieutenancy, in
the 82nd, with which regiment he served in America during the revolutionary war. In 1783, when the peace took place, he was reduced, and
soon after took his seat in Parliament for the borough of Lanark, &c. by
the interest of the Duke of Hamilton, to whom his father was tutor.
In 1787 or 1788 he obtained the majority of the 4th battalion of the
60th regiment, when he negotiated an exchange into his old corps, the
51st. In 1790 he succeeded, by purchase, to the lieutenant-colonelcy,
and went the following year to Gibraltar with it. After some other
movements, he was sent to Corsica, where General Charles Stuart, having
succeeded to the command of the army in 1794, appointed Colonel
Moore to that of the reserve, on which occasion he particularly distinguished himself at the siege of Calvi. In 1795 he returned to England, and was immediately appointed a brigadier-general in the West
Indies, where he served under Sir Ralph Abercromby. That discerning
veteran soon discovered his worth, and employed him in every arduous
and difficult service which occurred. When Sir Ralph was afterwards
appointed commander of the forces in Ireland, he particularly requested
that Brigadier-General Moore might be put upon the staff in that country, which was accordingly done, and he accompanied Sir Ralph to Dublin on the 2nd of December 1797. During the period immediately
preceding the rebellion in 1798, General Moore had an important command in the South of Ireland, and continued to serve there till the latter
end of June 1799 when he was ordered to return to England. This was

for the purpose of accompanying Sir Ralph Abercromby to Holland, on the expedition which sailed to that country in August, to rescue it from the tyranny of France. During that unsuccessful campaign, General Moore greatly distinguished himself. He was twice wounded in the hand, and in the thigh. He received a musket ball through his face, by which he was disabled, and forced to be removed from the scene of action. Being, however, of an excellent constitution, and temperate habits, his wounds closed in the course of a few weeks, and in 1800 he was once more appointed to co-operate with his old commander and steady friend, Sir Ralph Abercromby. He accompanied him to Egypt as one of his major-generals, and throughout the whole of that arduous service evinced, in the highest degree, personal intrepidity and military science. In the memorable action of the 21st of March, which proved fatal to Sir Ralph Abercromby, General Moore also received a wound in the leg, and towards the close of the battle had his horse killed under him. When the conflict was over, and not till then, he suffered his wound to be dressed. Finding, however, from the report of the surgeon, that it would be some time before he could resume his duties, he went on board the Diadem troop-ship. Here he was confined till nearly the middle of May, when he was removed to Rosetta, for the benefit of a change of air. His sufferings were very severe, the ball having passed between the two bones of his leg. At length, however, he began to recover, and was ultimately enabled to serve again with the army until after the surrender of Alexandria. He then returned to England, and was rewarded with the honor of knighthood, and the order of the Bath.

On the breaking out of the war, after the peace of the Amiens, he was not actively employed till 1808, when he was appointed to the chief command of the army intended to co-operate with the Spanish nation in resisting the usurpation of Buonaparte. After the liberation of Portugal, which was the result of the battle of Vimiera, the British government directed a force to assemble under Sir John Moore at Valladolid. This force was to be composed of 20,000 men from the army at Lisbon, and of 13,000 from England to be disembarked at Corunna under Sir David Baird. The latter arrived in Spain in the middle of October (1808); but the force at Lisbon was not prepared to move till the end of the same month.

The disastrous campaign that followed cannot be minutely traced. Sir John Moore was fatally deceived, as to the real resources and dispotion of the Spanish people, and had he not exercised the utmost prudence he would have become the victim of positive treachery. He was opposed to Buonaparte, who commanded the French army in person; but so skilful were his movements, so judicious were his plans, considering the unexpected embarrassments of his situation, that even Buonaparte himself praised him in one of his bulletins.

The troops of Sir John Moore did not amount to more than 27,000, while those of the French, on the lowest calculation, were 70,000. With such a disparity of force, it is more to be wondered at that he was enabled to retreat upon Corunna in such good order as he confessedly did, than that he should be forced to retreat at all.

The situation of Corunna, on the narrow neck of a promontory, and defended by a strong citadel, presented a secure and favourable point for embarkation. This operation would have been effected without any further molestation from the enemy, had the transports been in readiness to receive the troops; but unfortunately, it was not known precisely upon what point the English army would retire, and the transports had assembled at Vigo. They afterwards sailed for Corunna, where they arrived about the 12th of January (1809), and the cavalry were immediately sent on board. It was then arranged that the whole army should withdraw and embark on the evening of the 16th, but on the morning of that day the enemy, 20,000 strong, suddenly appeared, and a strong column immediately attacked the village on the right.

The contest was obstinate. Early in the action Sir David Baird, leading on his division, had his arm shattered with a grape shot, and was forced to leave the field. At that instant the French artillery plunged from the heights, and the two hostile lines of infantry mutually advanced beneath a shower of balls. They were still separated from each other by stone walls and hedges. A sudden and very able movement of the British gave the utmost satisfaction to Sir John Moore who had been watching the manœuvre, and he cried out " that is exactly what I wished to be done." He then proceeded to the 42nd, and addressed them in these words, " Highlanders, remember Egypt !" The appeal was electrical. They rushed forwards, driving the French before them. He sent Captain

Hardinge to order up a battalion of guards to the left flank of the Highlanders, upon which the officer commanding the light company, conceiving that, as their ammunition was nearly expended, they were to be relieved by the guards, began to fall back : but Sir John, discovering the mistake, exclaimed, " My brave 42nd, join your comrades—ammunition is coming —and you have your bayonets !" They instantly obeyed, and moved forward. While the General was speaking, a cannon-ball struck him to the ground. He raised himself, and sat with an unaltered countenance looking most intently at the Highlanders, who were warmly engaged. Being assured by Captain Hardinge that they were advancing, his countenance immediately brightened. He was soon afterwards conveyed from the field, and General Hope assumed the command. The cannon-shot had carried away his left shoulder, and part of the collar bone, leaving the arm hanging by the flesh. The blood flowed fast, and Captain Hardinge in vain attempted to stop it with his sash. When he was being raised from the ground, his sword, hanging on the wounded side, touched his arm, and became entangled between his legs. Captain Hardinge perceived the inconvenience, and was in the act of unbuckling it from his waist, when he said, in his usual tone and manner, and in a very distinct voice, " it is as well as it is ; I had rather it should go out of the field with me."

As the soldiers were carrying him slowly along in a blanket, he made them turn him round frequently to view the field of battle, and to listen to the firing, and was pleased when the sound grew fainter. On his arrival at his lodgings he was in much pain. He could speak but little, but at intervals he said to Colonel Anderson, who for one and twenty years had been his friend and companion in arms, " Anderson, you know that I always wished to die this way !" He frequently asked, " are the French beaten ?"—and at length, when he was told they were defeated in every point, he said, " It is a great satisfaction for me to know we have beaten the French. I hope the people of England will be satisfied, I hope my country will do me justice." Having mentioned the name of his venerable mother, and the names of some other friends for whose welfare he seemed anxious to offer his last prayers, the power of utterance was lost, and he died in a few minutes without a struggle. He was buried in his uniform upon the ramparts of Corunna, where a grave had been prepared by a party of the 9th regiment; and a monument to his memory was afterwards raised by the Marquis of Romana, with an inscription engraven upon it, of which the following is a translation.

To the Glory
of His Excellency Sir John Moore,
K. B.
General in Chief of the British Army
in Spain,
and to that of his valiant soldiers.
SPAIN GRATEFUL!

A monument has also been erected in St. Paul's Cathedral, in consequence of an address to his Majesty by the House of Commons, and for which a suitable inscription was written by Dr. Parr.

The following exquisite lines were published soon after the death of this lamented hero. The author of them is not known: at least not generally. But from whatever pen they proceeded, they prove the author to have possessed the finest perception of simple and eloquent poetry. They are full of inspiration.

THE BURIAL OF SIR JOHN MOORE AT CORUNNA.

Not a drum was heard, not a funeral note,
As his corse to the ramparts we hurried;
Not a soldier discharged his farewell shot,
O'er the grave where our hero was buried.

We buried him darkly at dead of night,
The sods with our bayonets turning,
By the struggling moon-beams' misty light,
And the lanthorns dimly burning.

No useless coffin inclos'd his breast,
Nor in sheet nor in shroud we bound him —
But he lay like a warrior taking his rest
With his martial cloak around him!

Few and short were the prayers we said,
And we spoke not a word of sorrow;
But we stedfastly gazed on the face of the dead,
And we bitterly thought of the morrow.

We thought, as we hollow'd, his narrow bed,
And smooth'd down his lonely pillow,
That the foe and the stranger would tread o'er his head,
And we far away on the billow.

Lightly they'll talk of the spirit that's gone,
And o'er his cold ashes upbraid him ;
But nothing he'll reck, if they let him sleep on,
In the grave where a Briton has laid him.

Slowly and sadly we laid him down
From the field of his fame fresh and gory ;
We carv'd not a line—we rais'd not a stone,
But we left him alone with his glory !

We cannot better describe the character and talents of Sir John Moore, than in the emphatic language of His Royal Highness the Commander in Chief, who pronounced the following just and energetic eulogium upon him in the general orders which he issued to the army after its return from Spain.

"The life of Sir John Moore was spent among the troops. During the season of repose his time was devoted to the care and instruction of the officer and soldier. In war, he courted service in every quarter of the globe. Regardless of personal consideration, he esteemed that to which his country called him, the post of honor ! And, by his undaunted spirit, and unconquerable perseverance, he pointed the way to victory. His country, the object of his latest solicitude will rear a monument to his lamented memory ; and the commander in chief feels that he is paying the best tribute to his memory, in thus holding him up as an example to the army."

Description of the Medal.

Obverse.—Head of Sir John Moore, by Mills.

Reverse.—A British soldier protecting the fallen body of Sir John Moore, who fell while heroically and successfully covering, from the attacks of the French, the retreat of his army from Corunna. This is by a celebrated Italian Medallist, and is considered one of the very best in the Series.

No. XV.

PASSAGE OF THE DOURO.

Sir Arthur Wellesley having been appointed to resume the command of the British army in Portugal, after the Convention of Cintra, he landed at Lisbon on the 22d of April, 1809. In the interval between those two events, the disastrous expedition of Sir John Moore had taken place, which ended in the retreat upon Corunna, and the lamentable death of that most gallant officer. Early in the month of March, the French army, under Marshal Soult, entered the province of Tras os Montes, and on the 26th of the same month appeared before the town of Oporto. On the 27th and 28th an attack was made, but without any decisive success. On the 29th however, owing to the mistrust of the Portuguese in their officers, he succeeded in forcing their lines, and entered the town with little loss.

The first object of Sir Arthur Wellesley, therefore, was, to rescue Oporto from the dominion of the enemy. Accordingly, on the 2d of May, only ten days after his landing at Lisbon, he quitted that city and proceeded northwards. The combined English and Portuguese army was stationed at Coimbra, where he reviewed it on the 6th of May, and on the 7th put it in motion. The infantry of the army was formed into three divisions. On the 10th the cavalry and advanced guard crossed the Vouga with the intention to surprise and cut off four regiments of French cavalry and a battalion of infantry and some artillery. The latter part of the enterprise was unsuccessful; but the superiority of the British cavalry was evident throughout the day, and we took their cannon and some prisoners from them, while the advanced guard took up a position at Oliviera.

On the 11th the army came up with the advanced guard of the enemy, consisting of about 4000 infantry and some squadrons of cavalry, strongly posted on the heights above Grijon. The enemy's left flank was turned

L

by a well executed movement on the part of General Murray, with Brigadier General Langworth's brigade of the Hanoverian legion; while the 16th Portuguese regiment of Brigadier General Stewart's brigade attacked their right, and the flank companies of the 29th, 43d, and 52d of the same brigade, under Major Way, attacked the infantry in the woods and villages in their centre. The result of this action was, that the enemy were defeated with considerable loss; they fell back towards Oporto, crossed the river Douro on the night of the 11th, and destroyed the bridge of boats.

As it was important, with a view to ulterior operations, that Sir Arthur should pass the Douro immediately, he collected with infinite labor and amazing celerity, the requisite number of boats, and on the following day his army crossed the river. This passage of the Douro, in the face of an enemy greatly superior in number, is justly reckoned among the most brilliant exploits of this great General. It would be impossible, indeed, to imagine any military operation displaying greater skill and genius; nor could the dauntless intrepidity, the unwearied perseverance, and resistless energy of the troops, be exceeded. They had made a forced march of above 80 miles from Coimbra in three days and a half. The current of the Douro is very rapid, and the opposite banks, which are high and steep, were in possession of the enemy. The passage was effected at the ferry of Ovintas, about four miles above Oporto. The enemy took no notice of our collection of boats, nor of the embarkation of the troops, till after the 1st battalion of the Buffs were landed, and had taken up their position under the command of Lieutenant General Sir Edward Paget. They then commenced an attack upon them with a large body of cavalry, infantry, and artillery, under the command of Marshal Soult, which that corps most gallantly sustained till they were supported, successively by the 48th and 60th regiments, belonging to General Hill's brigade, and afterwards by the first battalion of detachments belonging to General Stewart's brigade. At this moment Lieutenant General Paget unfortunately was wounded, when the command of these gallant troops devolved upon General Hill. Sir Arthur Wellesley, alluding to this accident in his dispatch, says, " In Lieutenant General Paget I have lost the assistance of a friend who had been most useful to me in the few days which had elapsed since he had joined the army." Although the French made repeated and fierce attacks upon our troops, they could produce no impression. The men stood with immoveable fortitude, and repelled every assault of the enemy. At length General Murray, by a masterly movement, having appeared on the left flank of the French, and General Sherbrooke on the right, with the brigade of Guards and the 29th regiment, the whole of the enemy's forces retired in the utmost confusion, leaving behind them five pieces of cannon, eight ammunition tumbrils, and many prisoners. Their loss in killed and wounded was very great, and they left behind them, in Oporto, 700 sick and wounded. Towards these the humane attention of Sir Arthur was first directed, and he had scarcely assured himself of his victory, when he issued a proclamation to the inhabitants of Oporto, reminding them that the prisoners were now, by the laws of war, entitled to his protection, and requiring that they should be treated by the Portuguese with mercy and compassion. Incensed as they were against their merciless oppressors, beneath whose iron sway they had been some time, such an inhibition and such an appeal were necessary to secure them from all the horrors of a sanguinary recrimination. The country, indeed, was so hostile to the French, that they could not get any information of our movements. The advance from Coimbra, therefore, was quite unexpected, and the passage of the Douro so little anticipated, that when Soult fled from Oporto, his dinner was actually preparing, and, it is said, was afterwards served up for Sir Arthur and his staff.

The results of this brilliant achievement were most decisive; for Soult hastily retreated by Braga, Salemondé, and Montalegre, into Gallicia, leaving behind him a fourth of his army, with the whole of their baggage and artillery, which strewed the roads in every direction along the line of their march. Sir Arthur having thus completely expelled the French from Portugal, marched his army southwards, and took up his quarters at Lisbon.

Description of the Medal.

Obverse.—Head of the Duke of Wellington.

Reverse.—The English passing the Douro. The difficulties of the passage are designated by the opposing attitude of the river Deity.

BATTLE OF TALAVERA.

THIS battle followed close upon the expulsion of the French from Portugal, by the occupation of Oporto. In the beginning of the month of July (1809) Marshal Victor broke up from his cantonments, and retreated from Truxillo by the bridges of Almarez and Arzibispo, across the Tagus, to Talavera de la Reyna. In this movement he was closely followed by Cuesta, as far as Las Casas del Puerto de Mirabete, who occupied a position here, with the main body of his army, while the Duke D'Albuquerque, with the advance of the Spaniards, was detached to the bridge of Arzibispo. Sir Arthur Wellesley, who had remained at Lisbon, anxiously awaiting the opportunity to commence offensive operations, now put the British force in motion, which once more entered Spain. His whole force amounted to about 20,000 men, and on the 17th and 18th of July they crossed the river Tieter, by a fine iron bridge, which had been thrown over it by the Spaniards. On the 20th the British and Spanish armies formed a junction at Oropesa, and on the 22d marched for Talavera. Some skirmishing took place between the rear guard of the enemy and our advanced guard, but nothing occurred of any moment.

Joseph Buonaparte, who styled himself king of Spain, had concentrated the whole of his disposable force by the 26th, between Torrijos and Toledo. It amounted to nearly 50,000 men, consisting of the corps of Marshal Victor, General Sebastiani, 9,000 of Joseph's Guards, and the garrison of Madrid. With these corps, aided by Marshal Jourdan, and their respective commanders, Joseph advanced the same day to Torrijos, and drove in the advanced guard of Cuesta, who retreated in a disorderly manner across the Alberche. It was now obvious that the enemy intended to try the result of a general action, for which the best position appeared to be in the neighbourhood of Talavera.

The position occupied by the allied British and Spanish army extended nearly three miles. The right flank was protected by the Tagus, and the left rested on a height which commanded the greater part of the field of battle. On the left of the position was a valley, running between the height and the mountains, which took the direction of Escalona. The Spanish army was posted on the right in two lines. The town of Talavera, in part surrounded with old walls, was occupied by a division of their troops. This part of the ground was covered with olive-trees, and much intersected by banks and ditches.

It was about two o'clock, on the 27th of July 1809, when the enemy appeared in strength, on the left bank of the Alberche, and manifested a disposition to attack General Mackenzie's division, which was placed as an advanced post, in a wood on the right of the Alberche. This attack was made before they could be withdrawn; but the troops, in the plain between Talavera and the wood, withdrew in good order, though not without some loss, particularly the 2nd battalion 87th regiment, and the 2nd battalion 31st regiment, in the wood. Upon this occasion, the steadiness and discipline of the 45th regiment and the 5th battalion of the 60th obtained the marked approbation of Sir Arthur Wellesley; as did also the masterly manner in which Major General Mackenzie withdrew his advanced guard.

As the day proceded, the enemy appeared in large numbers on the right of the Alberche, and it was evidently his intention to make a general attack on the combined army, which commenced in the dusk of the evening by a cannonade on the left of our position, and by an attempt, with his cavalry, to overthrow the Spanish infantry posted on the right. This attempt, however, totally failed. Early in the night, he pushed a division along the valley, on the left of the height occupied by General Hill, of which he gained a momentary possession, but he was instantly attacked by that General, and the position was recovered in a most gallant manner. This attack was repeated, during the night, and at day-light, on the morning of the 28th, but the enemy were both times repulsed by Major General Hill.

About noon a general attack was made by the enemy's whole force upon that part of the position which was occupied by the British army. In consequence of the repeated attempts upon the height which was on the left of the British, Sir Arthur Wellesley placed two brigades of cavalry in the valley, through which those attempts were made, and

supported them in the rear by the Duke D'Albuquerque's division of
Spanish Cavalry. The enemy then placed light infantry in the range of
mountains on the left of the valley, and the general attack began by the
march of several columns of infantry into the valley, with a view to obtain
possession of the heights occupied by Major General Hill. These columns
were immediately charged, in the most intrepid manner, by the 1st German
light dragoons, and the 2nd dragoons, under the command of General
Anson, directed by Lieutenant General Payne, and supported by General
Fane's brigade of heavy cavalry. This charge had the effect of frustrating
the enemy's plans, but the 23rd dragoons sustained considerable loss.

The next effort, on the enemy's side, was to force the position of General
Campbell, which was in the centre of the combined armies, and on the
right of the British. This, had it been successful, would probably have
determined the fate of the day, but General Campbell gallantly repulsed
his antagonists, supported by the King's regiment of Spanish cavalry, and
two battalions of Spanish infantry. He not only drove them back, but
he captured some of their cannon. At the same time that this attack was
made, a similar one was carried into execution against Lieutenant General
Sherbrooke's division, which was stationed on the left and centre of the first
line of the British army. It was in vain, however, that the enemy attempted
to penetrate our position. The cool, steady, and fearless character of the
British soldiers defied all the impetuous onsets of the French; and when
the latter approached close enough, the bayonet, that formidable weapon,
when wielded by a vigorous arm and undaunted heart, drove them back
with dismay. The enemy, finding themselves thus foiled on every side,
and having vainly made a desperate attack with the whole of their troops,
now determined upon a retreat across the Alberche, which was conducted,
however, in the most regular order, during the night.

The loss sustained by the French, in this battle, was estimated at 10,000
in killed, wounded, and prisoners, besides twenty pieces of cannon, ammunition tumbrils, &c. &c. " I am informed," said Sir Arthur, in his dispatch, " that entire brigades of infantry have been destroyed; and, indeed,
the battalions that retreated were much reduced in numbers." Generals
Lapisse and Morlet were killed; Generals Sebastiani and Boulet wounded.
Our own loss was considerable. The army, which entered the field above
18,000 effective men, with 30 pieces of cannon, lost, in the two days, 34

officers, 767 men, killed; 195 officers, 3,718 men wounded; 9 officers, 644 men missing; making a total of 5,367. Among those who were killed, were Major General Mackenzie, Brigadier General Langworth, of the King's German Legion, and Brigade Major Becket, of the Guards.

History does not present many harder fought battles than that of Talavera. The ground on which the British were posted was well chosen, and the troops were distributed with infinite judgment. The praise of these arrangements belonged exclusively to Sir Arthur Wellesley, but the meanest soldier in his camp might justly claim his share of that glory which the cool, steady, and disciplined bravery of the army achieved. When, indeed, we consider how very inefficiently Sir Arthur was supported in his operations by the Spaniards, and that, to use his own words, " the attacks of the enemy were principally, if not entirely, directed against the British troops," who had to fight against double their number, it is impossible not to feel the highest admiration at that dauntless spirit which not only resisted, but finally subdued such fearful odds.

The victory of Talavera, for such we shall presume to call it, in defiance of that military special pleading which would argue merely on the result, not the valour and generalship shewn, obtained for Sir Arthur his elevation to the peerage. On the 26th of August 1809, he was created Viscount Wellington of Talavera and of Wellington, and Baron Douro of Wellesley, in the county of Somerset. The French claimed the triumph on this occasion, a circumstance which is alluded to in the reverse of this medal. Upon this claim, however, it will be sufficient to observe, that though eventually the British army retreated to the confines of Portugal, yet the French retreated *first*, and they were completely repulsed and driven back in all their attacks.

DESCRIPTION OF THE MEDAL.

OBVERSE.—Marshal Wellington, by Mills.

REVERSE.—This victory, being rather indecisive, is expressed by the British Lion and the French Eagle on each side of the Genius of Victory. Though the French retreated, they claim the victory at Talavera. This is expressed by their endeavouring to seize the Laurel, which is already received by the British Lion from the hand of Victory.

No. XVII.

TORRES VEDRAS.

WHEN Lord Wellington fell back after the battle of Busaco (which was fought on the 27th September 1810), followed by the enemy in great force, he adopted a plan for securing his own army, and harassing the hostile one, which, however it might be lamented on the score of humanity, was admirably conceived, as a military stratagem. The greater part of the inhabitants in the different places through which the allied forces passed accompanied them in their retreat, carrying with them, at the same time, as much of private wealth as they could remove. All that remained which could be of the smallest use to the invaders was entirely destroyed, and the whole country rendered a barren and unproductive desert. Massena and his army soon began to feel the effects of this lamentable, but necessary desolation. In an intercepted letter to Berthier, he said, " the enemy burns and destroys every thing as he evacuates the country. He forces the inhabitants to abandon their houses on pain of death. Coimbra, a town of 20,000 inhabitants, is deserted. We find no provisions. The army is subsisted on Indian corn and vegetables which we find remaining on the ground." This picture was not overcharged; — every soul in Coimbra fled, leaving it literally a desert. The orders of the regency, indeed, were positive, for all to leave their houses, carry off all their goods or destroy them, and suffer nothing to fall into the hands of the enemy. The distress and misery that followed defy description; — weeping mothers were seen hurrying along with their screaming infants; young and interesting females, also bathed in tears, formed part of the melancholy procession; while the men, old and young, some vowing eternal vengeance against their ruthless destroyers, — others, wrapped in silent anguish at the total loss and ruin of all they possessed, mingled

XVII

XVIII

XIX

XX

London, Pub. July 1st 1820, by Henry Colburn & Co. Conduit Street.

their execrations and sighs with the tears and wailings of the women and children.

Buonaparte, incensed at a measure which so materially embarrassed the operations of his army, issued an acrimonious attack upon it in the " Moniteur." He was compelled, however, to applaud what he affected to condemn for its inhumanity. " The obstacles which the army of Portugal has met with," said he, " arise from an inactive system of defence, *profoundly combined*, and which has been carried into execution with a singular degree of barbarity, unknown in our European wars, happily for the honour and humanity of nations." It was amusing to read this burst of sensibility from a man who never suffered his own career to be checked —never for a moment—by any feeling that bore the faintest resemblance to mercy and humanity. The simple fact was, that Buonaparte and his generals had mistaken the character of Wellington. They considered him an ardent, active general in the day of battle, and so eager for fighting, that he did not always calculate his resources and strength. They never once suspected that he was equally prepared, as occasion might serve, to conquer with the rapidity of a Cæsar, or to oppose a Fabian policy, while waiting for the moment of action.

The object of Lord Wellington in this campaign was, to defend Portugal, and, at the same time, to occupy a considerable French force, which would otherwise have been employed in Spain. When Massena pursued the allied army after the battle of Busaco, he confidently anticipated that the British were flying to their ships off Lisbon : but when, on the 14th October 1810, he arrived in front of the lines of TORRES VEDRAS, and beheld, in person, the fortified position, he found, too late, the fatal error into which he had been betrayed by the superior military genius of Lord Wellington. This grand position of the allied army, in the selecting and fortifying of which Lord Wellington displayed such consummate sagacity, formed a line of strongly defended heights, extending from Alhambra on the Tagus, to Torres Vedras, about thirty miles from Lisbon, and from thence to the mouth of the Sissandro. Behind these were two other lines of trenches and redoubts, extending from Ericeyra and Mafra, on the sea, to the Tagus. One of these, which was next to the

M

fortified line of Torres Vedras, might be defended by 20,000 men; the other, which was nearer Lisbon, by half that number. On these was planted an immense power of heavy artillery; and besides this triple line, redoubts were raised at Peniche, Obidos, and other places. Many of the hills were fortified. On the left of the position the whole of the coast from Vimiera to the mouth of the Tagus, was studded with redoubts, mounted with heavy artillery. On the right, the banks of the Tagus were flanked by our armed boats. Mines, also, ready to spring, were formed in various places. In short, the whole country, from Lisbon almost to the Mondego, appeared like one fortification, in the shape of a crescent. Within the lines of Torres Vedras, Ericeyra, and Mafra, defended by from 70 to 80,000 fighting men, the allies had collected all the produce of the country through which they had retreated. With Lisbon, too, in their rear, they were abundantly supplied with every thing they wanted.

The sufferings of the French army while they remained before this impregnable position, were of the most appalling character. Yet they endured them for several months, and it was not till the 5th March 1811 that Marshal Massena, finding his magazines nearly exhausted, and his foragers meeting with no success, although detached sometimes twenty leagues, broke up with his army, and began his retreat. Lord Wellington immediately put his troops in motion, and closely pursued the enemy, till he had fairly driven them once more beyond the confines of Portugal. Such was the auspicious termination of a plan, which was greatly conceived and inflexibly executed; a plan, too, which in its consequences may be said to have involved the salvation of Europe. It was after Wellington quitted the lines of Torres Vedras, that he commenced his unbroken series of conquests which ceased not till he had planted the flag of England on the soil of imperial France. Had he been compelled to evacuate Portugal, and fly to his ships, who will be bold enough to say, that Europe would have been redeemed from the bondage of Napoleon?

DESCRIPTION OF THE MEDAL.

OBVERSE.—Marshal Wellington, in his tent, and in the dress of a Roman general, meditating on his future operations. He is compared on this classical obverse to the celebrated Roman general Fabius, who, by protracted delay and avoiding to fight, eventually defeated the greatest general of antiquity—Hannibal ; and was therefore called Fabius Cunctator, or Fabius the Delayer.

REVERSE.—A personification of the river Tagus, near which was the British army at Torres Vedras, represented by the tents. The orange-tree is a significant indication of Portugal, thus protected by the British.

No. XVIII.

BATTLE OF ALBUERA.

ON the 12th of May, 1811, while Marshal Beresford was occupied in besieging the strongly fortified town of Badajos, he received information from General Blake of the advance of Soult, from Seville, with above 20,000 men, for the purpose of raising that siege. Accordingly the siege was raised, and the stores and artillery removed on the night of the 14th under protection of General Cole's division. The army marched to Valverde, and united with a corps of Spaniards under Generals Castanos, Blake and Ballasteros, after which the whole took post, to give battle to the advancing force, and prevent any supplies being thrown into Badajos.

The position selected for the combined armies was behind the little river Albuera, where the roads leading from Seville to Olivenza and Badajos separate, after crossing the river by a bridge close to the river of Albuera. The river of that name empties itself into the Guadiana, and the village is on its left bank. The ground on the west side rises in gentle swells and easy slopes. On the summit of this rise, and nearly parallel to the river, the army was formed, its left having the village of Albuera in front, and the banks of the river being a further defence. The right had no particular *appui*.

On the night of the 15th May, Marshal Soult took post on some woody hills, with 20,000 infantry, and 600 cavalry, and 40 pieces of cannon. Marshal Beresford, to oppose him, had two divisions of British and Portuguese, one division of Portuguese, and 14,000 Spanish troops, composing a body of 27,000 infantry, 2000 cavalry, and 32 pieces of cannon.

The Spaniards were formed on the right in two lines. General Stewart's division was in the centre, and General Hamilton's Portuguese division on the left. General Cole's division and a Portuguese brigade formed a second line in rear of the centre. The village of Albuera was occupied by a brigade of light infantry under General Alten, and the cavalry under General Lumley were posted to cover the right flank of the Spaniards.

At eight o'clock, on the morning of the 16th a heavy French column marched out of the wood, directing its course on the village of Albuera, as if to attack the left of the allies; but while every eye was directed to that column, which, in reality was only a feint, the main body of the enemy, under cover of the wood to the right, crossed the Albuera, and began to ascend the heights on the right of the Spaniards unopposed. As soon as this movement could be distinctly ascertained, Marshal Beresford gave the Spanish troops a new *alignement* fronting their original flank, and threw back the right of his reserve, the better to support them.

The enemy commenced his attack at nine o'clock, directing his main effort against the Spaniards, who, after a strong and gallant resistance, were driven back by superior numbers. The heights which the enemy had thus gained, raked and entirely commanded the whole position of the combined army, while its rear was further threatened by a wide movement of the enemy's cavalry, round the right flank. The issue of the contest, therefore, depended on recovering the ground which the Spaniards had lost, and General Stewart's brigade was ordered forward for that purpose. At this moment, a heavy rain with a thick mist came on and obscured the combatants from each other. Hence, when the leading brigade of the division was in the act of charging the enemy, some squadrons of Polish lancers wheeled unperceived into their rear, fell unexpectedly on their right flank, and made all but the left battalion prisoners.

The day now appeared lost, when Major General the Hon. William Stewart, with the remainder of his division, and General Cole, with part of his division, immediately moved forward in line, charged the enemy before their formation was complete, drove them off the hill with prodigious slaughter, and secured the victory to the allies. Never was there a more fierce and desperate trial of individual and collective bravery. Major General Houghton (who, in the act of cheering his men on to the charge, fell pierced with wounds) and many other distinguished officers, lost their lives, while whole ranks of men were observed, after the combat, extended on the ground in the order in which they had fought. The Polish lancers did dreadful execution in this onset. They galloped about in all directions, spearing many of the wounded men and their defenceless supporters. One of them even charged Marshal Beresford himself, who, grappling with him threw him from his horse, when the stroke of a sabre from an orderly dragoon finished his career.

After the enemy had been thus repulsed in his principal attack, he still continued, for a short time, near the village, on which, however, he never could make any impression. The French officers made many efforts, but in vain, to rally their men. The action, which commenced at nine o'clock in the morning, continued without interruption till two, when the enemy being completely driven across the Albuera, there were only skirmishing and cannonading for the remainder of the day; and on the night of the 17th Soult commenced his retreat on Seville, pursued by the allied cavalry, who, in a gallant affair at Usagre, made some prisoners.

The loss of the enemy on this hard contested day was estimated at upwards of nine thousand men. The British and Portuguese also suffered severely, having 1,000 killed, 3000 wounded, and 570 made prisoners. The Spaniards had not above 2,000 in killed and wounded.

On the 18th the infantry resumed its ground before Badajos, and Marshal Beresford had the satisfaction to find that Soult had been unable to communicate with the garrison, and that, consequently, the object of his giving battle to the French at Albuera had been completely attained.

DESCRIPTION OF THE MEDAL.

OBVERSE.—A fine head of the commander in this battle, Marshal Beresford, by Webb.

REVERSE.—The fierce charge of the Polish Lancers successfully resisted by the British Infantry. The carnage in this battle pourtrayed by the figure prostrate in death.

LIEUTENANT-GENERAL SIR THOMAS PICTON, K. B.

THIS distinguished officer entered the army in September 1771, when he obtained an ensigncy in the 12th regiment of foot. He was afterwards (1776) promoted to the rank of lieutenant in the same regiment, and served with it in Gibraltar, under General Sir Robert Boyd and Lord Heathfield, till the year 1778. He next obtained the command of a company in the 75th regiment, and remained a captain for the period of sixteen years, from 1778 to 1794. In 1783 he commanded the 75th, then quartered in Bristol, and quelled a mutiny which broke out in that regiment, and which, from the character it had assumed threatened the most disastrous consequences. His conduct on this occasion was so exemplary, and the services he rendered were considered of so much importance, that he received the royal approbation through the then commander-in-chief, Field-Marshal Conway.

In the year 1794 he embarked for the West Indies, where Sir John Vaughan, the commander-in-chief on that station, gave him a majority in the 68th regiment, and made him his aide-de-camp. Two years afterwards, he was preparing to return to England, but Sir Ralph Abercromby, who had arrived in the West Indies, requested him to remain, hoping, as he said, " to give him an opportunity of returning in a way more agreeable to him." He accordingly embarked with Sir Ralph in the expedition against St. Lucie, where the general announced in public orders " that all orders coming through Lieutenant-colonel Picton should be considered as the orders of the commander-in-chief." On the capture of this island, the general recommended him for the lieutenant-colonelcy of the 68th regiment. From St. Lucie, Lieutenant-colonel Picton sailed with Sir Ralph on the expedition to St. Vincent's, which was taken by storm. Upon the conclusion of this short campaign, he went with Sir Ralph to Martinique, and afterwards returned to England.

In 1797 he again sailed for the West Indies, under the command of Sir Ralph Abercromby, and arrived with him in Martinique. The expedition against Trinidad being at this time determined on, the armament sailed for that island in February 1797; and the conquest of the colony being completed, Lieutenant-colonel Picton was appointed Governor. When he waited upon Sir Ralph to return his acknowledgments, he said, with honourable frankness, " Lieutenant-colonel Picton, if I knew any officer who, in my opinion, could discharge the duties annexed to this situation better than you, to him would I have given it : there are no thanks due to me for it." From the period of its capitulation, to the year 1802, when the government of Trinidad was put in commission, Lieutenant-colonel Picton discharged the duties of governor and captain-general, and received the thanks of the different commanders-in-chief on the station, as well as the approbation of his Majesty's ministers. The subsequent transactions, in which Colonel Picton's character for humanity was so unjustly aspersed, are sufficiently known to the public. For a time, his name was loaded with obloquy, and he became the object of vulgar clamour; but the law, at last, in tardy reparation of his injuries, proclaimed his innocence, and vindicated his honour.

In 1809 (having been promoted to the rank of major-general the preceding year) he commanded a brigade at the siege of Flushing, of which fortress he was afterwards appointed governor. But he did not escape the fatal fever which committed such ravages in the British army, and he returned home alarmingly ill. His health was scarcely re-established when he was placed on the staff of the army in the Peninsula. He joined the Marquis of Wellington, and partook largely of all the glory which attended the campaigns of that renowned commander. There is no name indeed which appears more frequently, and always with honour, in the dispatches of Wellington than that of Picton. He commanded the gallant third division, which so eminently distinguished itself throughout the Peninsular war, and whose very name became a terror to the enemy.

In the memorable siege of Badajoz, perhaps the most heroical and murderous assault recorded in the military annals of any nation, General Picton manifested consummate skill and intrepidity. This tremendous conflict took place on the 6th of April 1812. The Marquis of Wellington

having reduced the strong fortress of Ciudad Rodrigo, in the north, determined to follow up his success by the still more daring attempt of cap-
turing Badajoz in the south. This garrison had already resisted more
than one fierce attack on the part of the British; and on reconnoitering it
now, it was found that it had been materially strengthened since the assault
of the preceding summer. The garrison was ample and select, and commanded by General Philippon, whose two former successful defences had
inspired all around him with confidence. Wellington, however, laid
down a most admirable plan, which was nobly executed by those to whom
it was entrusted.

General Picton was ordered to attack the castle of Badajoz by escalade,
with the third division, while a detachment from the guard, in the
trenches, under Major Wilson of the 48th regiment, was to attack the
ravelin of San Roque upon his left. The fourth division, under General
Colville, and the light division, under Colonel Barnard, were ordered to
attack the breaches that had been effected in the bastions of La Trinidad
and Santa Maria, and in the curtain by which they were connected. In
furtherance of this plan, the 5th division were to occupy the ground
which the 4th and light divisions had occupied, and Lieutenant General
Leith was to make a false attack upon the outwork called Pardelleras.
Another false attack was to be made on the works of the fort towards the
Guadiana, with the left brigade of the division under Major General
Walker, which he was to turn into a real attack, if circumstances should
prove favourable.

These were the principal dispositions; and, every thing being arranged,
the assault commenced at 10 o'clock at night, General Picton's division
preceding, by a few minutes, the attack by the remainder of the troops.
They were discovered on reaching the glacis, and instantly a destructive
fire was opened upon them. The men, however, undauntedly advanced,
leaped into the covered way, where the palisadoes had been purposely destroyed by the batteries, and quickly descended into the ditch. The enemy
had the whole front doubly manned, and the summit of the breaches
covered with *chevaux de frise.* Confident in their situation, and well
provided with every means of annoyance, they poured down one incessant fire on their intrepid assailants, who made many gallant, but un-

N

connected efforts to force the breaches. Many of the officers even led parties of their men to grapple with the spears fixed on the crest, but unfortunately they were never strong enough to remove them. These efforts were continued for two hours, when the majority of the officers being disabled, and success appearing hopeless, a part of the troops were withdrawn, to be re-organized for fresh efforts as soon as day should dawn.

General Picton, in the quarter where he was engaged, met with a similar resistance from the garrison, and his division suffered severely. But he still persevered, and bringing forward fresh assailants, as fast as the preceding fell, he at length established a footing on the top of the wall, where with his own hands he planted the British standard. The defenders were alarmed; other points were quickly forced, and the assailants became masters of the post. Similar success attended the gallant efforts of General Leith, at the point allotted to his division, while General Walker's brigade, sweeping round the ramparts, fell unexpectedly on the troops stationed for the defence of the breaches, and soon dispersed them. The garrison, being thus overpowered, were made prisoners,—a signal instance of British humanity. By the laws of war, they might have put every French soldier to the sword. The governor and staff, with a few men, took refuge in Fort Christoval, on the opposite side of the river, till the tumult had subsided, when they sent their submission, augmenting the number of captives to nearly 4,000. The besiegers lost 59 officers, and 744 men killed; and had 258 officers, and 2,600 men wounded,

A more daring enterprize was, perhaps, never achieved. Many thousand shells and hand-grenades, numerous bags, filled with powder, every kind of burning composition and destructive missile had been prepared, and placed behind the parapet of the whole front. These, under an incessant roll of musquetry, were hurled into the ditch, without intermission, for upwards of two hours, giving to its surface an appearance of vomiting fire, and producing sudden flashes of light more vivid than day. In defiance, however, of such terrific means of defence, English soldiers marched up to the breaches, and finally vanquished the garrison.

The Earl of Liverpool, in moving the thanks of the House of Lords to the army for this gallant exploit, observed, " the conduct of Lieutenant General Picton had inspired a confidence in the army, and exhibited an example of science and bravery which had been surpassed by no other officer; his exertions in the attack on the 6th could not fail to excite the most lively feelings of admiration."

It may be observed, in conclusion, that Sir Thomas Picton fell gloriously at the battle of Waterloo, while leading his men to one of the most decisive charges against the enemy that was made during that arduous day. His loss was sincerely deplored by his country, by his friends, by his brave soldiers, and by none more than by the illustrious chief with whom he had shared the dangers and the honours of many a hard-fought field.

DESCRIPTION OF THE MEDAL.

OBVERSE.—Bust of General Picton, in his military uniform.

REVERSE.—Badajoz was taken by storm, and particularly by the bravery and skill of General Picton, who escaladed and captured its castle, as is here described, by his planting the British standard on the walls, at the moment of his arrival on them.

GENERAL LORD HILL.

THIS distinguished commander, whose name and exploits are so intimately associated with the whole course of the Peninsular war, is the second son of Sir John Hill, Bart. of Hawkstone in the county of Shropshire. He entered the army at a very early age, and from merit rather than influence, soon passed through all the subordinate degrees of promotion. He accompanied the memorable expedition to Egypt, under Sir Ralph Abercromby, and on his return received the thanks of both Houses of Parliament, in conjunction with the rest of the army. But it was in Spain and Portugal (the theatre where so many of our victorious generals first displayed their warlike talents), that Sir Rowland Hill performed those numerous and brilliant achievements which induced his sovereign to reward them by patrician honours. In the sanguinary conflict at Talavera he eminently distinguished himself, and, after repulsing the French in repeated attacks, was wounded, though fortunately not very severely.

The merit of General Hill, in surprising the enemy at Arroyo des Molinos, in November 1811, was of so conspicuous a character, that it was specially noticed by his Royal Highness the Prince Regent in his speech to Parliament. " The successful and brilliant enterprise," said his Royal Highness, " which ended in the surprise, in Spanish Estremadura, of a French corps, by a detachment of the allied army under Lieutenant General Hill, is highly creditable to that distinguished officer, and the troops under his command, and has contributed materially to obstruct the designs of the enemy in that part of the Peninsula."

In the following year he performed that distinguished service at Almarez, which is commemorated in the present medal, and which confers the second title upon his peerage.

On the 8th of November 1813, he received the unanimous thanks of both Houses of Parliament, for the valour, steadiness, and exertion, so successfully displayed by him in repelling the repeated attacks made on the positions of the allied army by the whole French force, under Marshal Soult, between the 25th of July and the 3rd of August 1813. On the 18th of June, the following year, when a general peace had taken place, he received the freedom of the City of London, with a valuable sword, for his long and meritorious services. He had previously been elevated to the peerage (May 3rd 1814), by the title of Baron Hill of Almarez and Hawkstone, in the county of Shropshire, with an annuity of £2,000 per annum settled upon himself, and the two next successors to the Barony of Hill. His lordship has likewise attained many honorary distinctions on account of his conspicuous gallantry, being a G. C. B. K. T. S. K. M. T. and K. S. G. He is also a Lieutenant General in the army, Colonel of the 53d regiment of foot, and governor of Hull.

It now remains to narrate the particular exploit above mentioned.

At the commencement of the campaign in 1812, it was deemed of the highest importance by Lord Wellington, with a view to ulterior operations, that the communication between the French armies on the North and South of the Tagus should be rendered as tedious and difficult as possible. To accomplish this, it was necessary that the bridge of boats at Almarez should be destroyed, as it was their best and shortest line of communication. All the permanent bridges from Toledo downwards had already been destroyed by one or other of the belligerents in the course of the war, and the roads leading from them were scarcely practicable for carriages.

The French commanders were duly sensible of the importance of this bridge, as the link of mutual strength, security, and communication, and they had therefore surrounded it on both sides of the river with formidable enclosed works, having, in the interior of them, casemated and loop-holed towers. Sir Rowland Hill was employed to effect this arduous enterprise, and his corps broke up from Almandralejo on the 12th of May. Marching by Jaraciejo, it reached, on the 18th, the Sierra, between four and five miles from Almarez, on which the castle of Miravete stands. The French had put that post in a state of defence, and having connected it by a line of works with a fortified house on the opposite side of the main road, they raised a formidable barrier across the only communication by which artillery could be brought from the South against the works of the bridge. The enemy considered them perfectly secure from attack by any weapons of a less powerful description. Sir Rowland Hill, however, was of a different opinion, and finding that infantry could cross the Sierra by a tract leading through the village of Romanzorda, he left his artillery on the mountain, and at dark began to descend with a column of 2,000 men. The leading company arrived, at dawn of day, close to the principal fort, built upon a height a few hundred yards in advance of the *tête-du-pont;* but such were the difficulties of the road, that several hours passed away before the rear had closed. During this time, fortunately, a deep ravine concealed the troops from the view of those within the work, and the first discovery they made of their danger was on a desperate rush forward to the assault. Aware, however, from a feint which had been made on the works of Miravete, that an enemy was in the neighbourhood, the garrison was on the alert, and, opening a heavy fire, resisted with vigour the efforts made to push up the scarp. The moment, however, the first men gained a footing on the parapet, their firmness forsook them; they took to flight—abandoned the tower—and endeavoured to escape over the bridge through the *tête-du-pont.* The officer commanding the fort on the opposite bank immediately cut the bridge, and upwards of 250 of the fugitives were, in consequence, made prisoners. He even, in his fright, abandoned his post, and retired with his garrison to Talavera, for which conduct he was tried and shot. The whole of this formidable post on both sides of the river thus fell to the infantry alone, at the small loss of 33 killed, and 147 wounded. The entire establishment, with the great depot of stores it contained (with the exception of 13 pieces of cannon, of which the victors made prize), was the same day destroyed, and the troops immediately retired.

DESCRIPTION OF THE MEDAL.

OBVERSE.—Head of Lord Hill, inscribed, " LIEUTENANT GENERAL LORD HILL," done from a bust of his Lordship, by Hopper.

REVERSE.—An allegorical representation of the successful progress of the British Arms, under Lord Hill, at Almarez, where he assaulted and carried a strong fort at the approach to the bridge, and drove the French to the other side of the bridge, who abandoned there another strong fort. The bridge and forts were destroyed. The British Military power is here represented by the Goddess of War, Bellona; and its success by the Goddess of Victory, with her palm branch.

Pl. 6.

XXI

XXII

XXIII

XXIV

Normand. fils.

London, Pub. July 1st 1820, by Henry Colburn & Co. Conduit Street.

No. XXI.

BATTLE OF SALAMANCA.

THIS memorable conflict took place on the 22nd of July 1812, near the city from which it derives its name. Early on the morning of that day, the British army took up the ground in position, placing its right near the bold rocky heights called the Arapiles, and its left on the Tormes. The enemy were immediately in front, covered by a thick wood. They were commanded by Marshal Marmont.

About eight A. M. a French column rapidly advanced from this wood, and seized the outer and most extensive of those strong points, upon which the allies took possession of the others as quickly as possible. After a variety of evolutions and movements, Marshal Marmont appeared at last to have determined upon his plan, about two o'clock in the afternoon. Under cover of a very heavy cannonade which, however, did the British but little injury, he extended his left with great shew. This was an attempt to turn the position of the allies, whereby, with a force little superior to theirs, he acted on the circumference of an arc of one third greater extent than their line. Lord Wellington, who was eagerly watching for some false movement of his antagonist, instantly profited by this, and at once determined to become the assailant instead of continuing to act on the defensive.

He accordingly made the following disposition of this army. The 1st and light division, under Generals Campbell and Alten, were stationed to the left of the Arapiles heights, as the extreme left of the line : the divisions of Generals Cole and Leith were in two lines on the right of that point, with the divisions of Generals Clinton and Hope, and a body of Spaniards under Don Carlos de Espana, in column to support them. Major General Packenham's division, with a considerable body of cavalry, formed the extreme right. While these movements were in progress, the enemy made several unsuccessful endeavours to possess themselves of the village of Arapiles, situated between the two armies, and occupied by a detachment of the guards. The moment the formation of the army was completed, the attack commenced from the right. Major General Packenham with his division, supported by several squadrons of cavalry, under Major-General D'Urban, moved along a valley at a very quick rate, and crossed the extended left of the enemy almost before they were aware of the attempt. Nearly at the same time, General Cole's and Leith's divisions, supported by General Clinton's and Hope's, moved forward and attacked them in front, while a Portuguese brigade, under Brigadier-General Pack, advanced against the bold height of the Arapiles. General Packenham's division, with the cavalry, quickly overthrew the left of the French, and constantly bringing up their right, so as to out-flank the points on which they attempted to stand, drove them for a considerable distance from one height to another, and made above 300 prisoners.

Similar success attended the operations of Generals Cole and Leith, who were rapidly pursuing their objects along the crest of the enemy's position, when they were momentarily checked by a body of troops advancing on their left flank from the Arapiles height, which, from its great strength, the Portuguese had been unable to carry. Marshal Beresford, who was on the spot, changed the front of a brigade in reserve, which held in check the troops near the Arapiles till the arrival of General Clinton's division, when the French abandoned that important point, and the battle again became a series of triumphs. A charge of cavalry made by Sir Stapleton Cotton, in which the "noble officer" (as Lord Wellington termed him in his dispatch) General le Marchant fell, was eminently successful, and all the heights on which the enemy endeavoured to check our pursuit, were immediately carried.

The only appearance of equal resistance was displayed, for a short time, on the French right, where the fugitives, forced back from their left by the advance of General Packenham, attempted to reform, under protection of the troops which had retired in good order from the Arapiles. An attack in front, made by General Clinton, cost many men; but on a flank movement of General Cole, they hastily retired, and the allied troops pursued them till night as quickly as they could march. Never was an army more completely routed. Marshal Marmont and his second being disabled, the command of the French devolved upon General Clausel, who, as soon as it became dark, made a most rapid march to Alba de Tormes. The first and light divisions were ordered to the fort of Huerta, in expectation that the Spaniards would continue to hold the castle of Alba, and that consequently the retreat of the enemy must be by Huerta; but the French having contrived to dislodge the Spaniards from the castle, crossed the Tormes at that spot in the course of the night, and saved themselves from the further considerable loss which must otherwise have ensued. The next morning the main body of the allies advanced to Alba, where the cavalry crossed, and shortly afterwards came up with the rear guard of the fugitives. A brilliant charge was directed against them by General Bock, with a brigade of heavy dragoons of the German legion, in which numbers were sabred, and nine hundred made prisoners. Many others owed their safety to throwing away their arms, and scrambling over the enclosures. Lord Wellington followed the fugitives to Valladolid, which he entered on the 30th, but finding they continued in full retreat on Burgos, and that he had no chance of overtaking them, he re-crossed the Douro the next day.

The loss of the enemy in this sanguinary conflict was very great. Besides the numbers of dead and wounded, 7,000 prisoners were taken, eleven pieces of artillery, two eagles, and six colours. The allies had nearly 5,000 killed and wounded. Among the latter were five general officers, Beresford, Stapleton Cotton, Cole, Leith, and Alten. Sir Stapleton Cotton was unfortunately wounded by one of our own sentinels, after he had halted from the pursuit, owing to the darkness of the night.

Such was the battle of Salamanca, a battle which may rank with the noblest exploits recorded in history, whether we consider the decisive skill and dauntless energy with which it was fought, or the wisdom and promptitude that directed its operations. Undoubtedly Marmont committed a great blunder, but even when committed, and even when detected, it required no common portion of sagacity, no common effort of genius, to convert that blunder into the elements of a signal and glorious victory.

One of the more immediate results of this battle, was the entrance of

o

Lord Wellington into Madrid, on the 12th of August, Joseph and his army having precipitately abandoned the town, by the road of Toledo, on the approach of the allies.

———————

Description of the Medal.

Obverse. — The British armies displayed great courage in dislodging the French, under General Marmont, from their very advantageous positions on the heights. This is described by the British troops about victoriously to pursue the enemy, on whom the Goddess of War is hurling destruction : the back ground represents the Arapile mountains.

Reverse. — Entry of the British into Madrid. It was the result of this battle ; the inhabitants are represented honouring the conqueror, the Duke of Wellington, with garlands of flowers.

No. XXII.

BATTLE OF VITTORIA.

HAD the battle of Waterloo never been fought, the battle of Vittoria would have remained the greatest achievement, amid the many great achievements of the Duke of Wellington's life. It was himself, alone, who could win a brighter wreath of fame.

The campaign of 1813, from various causes not necessary to be here stated, began late. It was not till the middle of May that the main body of the allied army crossed the Douro, at various points between Lamego and the frontier, directing its march on Zamora, while Lord Wellington in person, with two divisions of infantry, a corps of Spaniards, and some cavalry, advanced by the direct road to Salamanca. This double movement completely concealed his projects, and deceived the enemy, who had no suspicion that the main force of the allies had been crossed over to their rear so expeditiously. The French officer who commanded in Salamanca, having barricadoed the bridge and the principal communications through the town, allowed himself to be so long amused by demonstrations of a front attack, that detachments crossed the Tormes above and below the place before he moved. He consequently lost part of his artillery and many men, and nothing but the exceedingly brave and steady conduct of the remainder enabled them to reach the Douro. The city of Salamanca was then occupied by General Fane, on the 26th of May.

The allied troops, marching on the north of the Douro, first met the enemy on the Esta; but although the banks were steep, and the current rapid, no opposition was offered to the passage. The French, on the contrary, were so alarmed at the unexpected appearance of such a considerable force, that they abandoned Zamora and Toro, destroying the bridges. At the latter place, on the 1st of June, the whole of the allied forces united, on the right of the Douro, and thus accomplished the first object of the campaign.

Joseph Buonaparte, on becoming acquainted with these movements, concentrated his troops on the main road to Burgos, along which are to be found many fine defensive positions. That road was consequently their vantage ground, and Lord Wellington, to force them to abandon it again manœuvred to the left, and marching on Palencia, approached so near the enemy's line of communication as to give them serious apprehensions for its preservation. On the 12th of June, a strong reconnoisance dislodged a French corps from the heights of Estapar, and threw them in confusion on Burgos, which a further demonstration to the left induced them to blow up with such precipitation that three or four hundred men perished by the explosion.

After this destruction of Burgos, the different divisions of the French army directed their march on Vittoria, while the allies, still moving to the left of the great road, crossed the Ebro, on the 13th of June, by the bridges of St. Martin and Fuente de Arenas, and on the 20th (after some skirmishing at St. Millan and Osma, with French detachments marching to join their main body,) assembled on the little river Bagas. They completely flanked the enemy's line of movement, and were only separated by a bold range of heights, of no great extent, from the plain of Vittoria their point of concentration.

Lord Wellington, the same evening, after a careful reconnoissance, made arrangements for a general action the following morning (June 21st), if the enemy should still remain in position. They did remain, but it was only to sustain so complete an overthrow and rout as were without a parallel, till the battle of Waterloo presented one.

On the morning of the 21st of June, the allied army was moved in three corps over the heights which separated them from the enemy. The right was commanded by Sir Rowland Hill, the centre by Sir Lowry Cole and Lord Dalhousie, and the left by Sir Thomas Graham.

The French rested with their right upon the heights which end at Pueble de Arlanzon, and extended from thence across the valley of Zadora, in front of the village of Arunez. With the right of their centre they occupied a height which commanded the valley of Zadora, and the right of the whole was stationed near Vittoria, destined to defend the passage of the Zadora, while in the rear of their left they had a reserve at the village of Gomecha.

The strength of the two armies was nearly equal. The different corps of the allies marched directly from the summit of the heights to their points of attack. The right under Sir Rowland Hill, became first engaged with the enemy's advance at La Puebla, and after a short resistance dislodged it from the mountains. Strong reinforcements, however, being sent immediately to its support, the contest was renewed, and continued for some time with much obstinacy. It was during this conflict that the Hon. Lieutenant Colonel Cadogan fell, whose death was graced in a manner worthy of the purest ages of chivalry. When it was found that he was mortally wounded the soldiers prepared to bear him off the field. " No," said the hero, " my death is now certain, and very near, suffer me to conclude my life with the pleasure of seeing the continuance of our triumph ; carry me to a height from whence I can observe it." He was obeyed ; and being placed against a tree he shortly afterwards expired.

The contest in this quarter soon terminated in favour of the British, who crossed the Zadora in pursuit of the fugitives, and attacked and gained possession of the village of Sabijuna de Alva, immediately in front of their left. This success depriving the centre of the French of their chief support, Sir Lowry Cole seized the favourable moment to cross the Zadora by some bridges, which through neglect had not been destroyed. He vigorously attacked that part of the enemy's position, and being promptly supported by Lord Dalhousie's division, they were driven back upon Vittoria.

In the mean time Sir T. Graham, who commanded the left of the army, now moved forward from Margina towards Vittoria, by the high road from that town to Bilboa. He shortly after drove the enemy's right from the heights above Abechucho, on which Joseph, seeing his communication with Bayonne nearly intercepted, marched a corps still farther to the right, to occupy the villages of Gamarra Major and Minor on the Zadora. The possession of these heights enabled him to dispute the passage of that river, and to cover the march of his convoys, and the retreat of his army. Sir Thomas Graham, therefore, dispatched the Spaniards under Longa to drive them from the one, and General Oswald's division to drive them from the other ; while, with the remainder of his corps, he attacked in person the village of Abechucho. Gamarra Major was carried at the point of the bayonet by the determined advance of General Robinson's brigade, and Abechucho by a less exertion after it had been for some time cannonaded.

The enemy, in order to recover the posts thus lost, collected a strong body of troops in the rear of Gamarra Major, which, though it failed in several bold attempts to retake the village, was too powerful for a single division to advance and attack. It prevented, therefore, General Oswald from immediately following up his first success; but, as soon as the allies had penetrated to the town of Vittoria, the corps which thus held him in check, fearing to be taken in the rear, retrograded. The division then crossed the Zadora, and possessed themselves of the high road to Bayonne, forcing back on Vittoria the right as well as the left and centre of the French. The only road open for retreat was that leading to Pamplona. The confusion among the different corps of the enemy, thus driven back upon each other, was exceedingly great, and, in a short time, the whole army became little better than one immense mob. The cavalry alone preserved some degree of order, and endeavoured to cover the retreat. The British made a most pressing advance. They did not allow the enemy a moment's delay; and 151 guns, 415 caissons, above 14,000 rounds of ammunition, and nearly 2,000,000 of musquet cartridges remained on the field! The French carried off with them only one gun and one howitzer, and the former was taken from them the following day. Of the more brilliant spoils of this hard fought day, were the colours of the 4th battalion of the 100th regiment, together with Marshal Jourdan's *baton*, who commanded, under Joseph, as Major General of the army. This trophy was taken by the 87th regiment.

The total loss sustained by the allied armies was 740 killed, and 4,170 wounded. The number of killed, wounded, and prisoners, of the French, was not in proportion to their loss of artillery and accompaniments, probably not exceeding 10,000. The small number of prisoners has been ascribed to the circumstance, that the victors were more eager to possess themselves of the spoils of the field, than to follow the panic-struck enemy. Those spoils were immense. Near Vittoria 2,000 carriages of different descriptions were abandoned, containing money, valuables, and all the royal establishment. Joseph, himself, only escaped being a prisoner, by quitting his vehicle and mounting a horse, at the moment that a squadron of British dragoons approached. Indeed, so little was this signal overthrow anticipated, that the wives of the courtiers and of the chief officers of state were obliged to seek safety in personal exertion, and some hundreds of terrified women and children fled over the fields, and subsequently accompanied the march of the army on foot.

Such was the battle of Vittoria. The triumph achieved was equal to that of Blenheim. There is no record of a veteran army, struck with a paralysis so destructive of its military powers by the mere force of that genius which confounded and assaulted them. There is no recorded instance of a body of 70,000 veterans, so reduced in one short hour, from the condition of a gallant army to that of a defenceless multitude.

DESCRIPTION OF THE MEDAL.

OBVERSE.—Duke of Wellington, in his Marshal's dress, ably executed by Mills.

REVERSE.—This beautiful reverse displays the Genius of War and Victory pursuing the French, who, in their precipitate flight, left in the possession of the British, King Joseph's valuable baggage, money, pictures, &c.

No. XXIII.

BATTLE OF THE PYRENEES.

THE decisive overthrow of the armies of France, in their total route at Vittoria, was an event which, while it inspired unbounded hopes in the bosoms of the victors, filled the vanquished with indescribable dismay. Buonaparte was at that time making a desperate struggle for his dominion n Germany; but sensible of the perils which threatened France on its southern frontiers, he despatched Soult to that quarter, armed with unusual powers. By an imperial decree of the 1st of July, he was declared Lieutenant de l'Empereur, and commander in chief of the armies in Spain, as if Buonaparte still possessed a really disposable and formidable force in that country. Soult arrived in the South on the 15th of July 1813, and the army having been joined by Clausel's corps and other reinforcements, was distributed into nine divisions of infantry, besides two divisions of dragoons, and one of light cavalry. There was also a large proportion of artillery. Soult loudly proclaimed his intention of carrying the war beyond the Ebro, and as a proof of his expectation of success, he collected cavalry and artillery, arms of little value for a struggle in the Pyrenees. His first enterprise was to relieve Pampeluna; and with that view he assembled, towards the end of July, a convoy of provisions and stores at St. Jean Pied de Port, concentrating the main body of his army in the environs of the town.

The operations which the allied army had to carry on, were at once complicated and hazardous. They had to attempt the defence of the passes of the Pyrenees, under the disadvantage of having two points to cover, sixty miles distant from each other; and they had, at the same time, two blockades to maintain, those of St. Sebastian and Pampeluna. To unite these four objects, the following dispositions were made by the Marquis of Wellington.

The besieging force at St. Sebastian, under Sir T. Graham, with its covering army (chiefly Spaniards) on the Bidassoa, formed the extreme left. A brigade of British infantry under General Byng, with a corps of Spaniards under Morillo in the pass of Ronscevalles, formed the extreme right, having as their support Sir Lowry Cole's division at Biscaret, in their immediate rear, and Sir T. Picton's division at Olaque. General Stewart's division with Silvierra's Portuguese division under Sir R. Hill were posted in the pass of Maya, about twenty miles on the left of Ronscevalles, having General Campbell's Portuguese brigade detached to Los Alduides. The light division under Baron C. Alten guarded the heights of St. Barbara, and Lord Dalhousie's division the Puerto de Echalar, intermediate points between the right and left; General Pack's division (the sixth) being in reserve at the interior pass of San Estevan. The Conde D'Abisbal with 10,000 Spaniards was charged with the blockade of Pampeluna.

Soult's arrangements were to attack on the same day, in force, the passes of Ronscevalles and Maya, the roads from which diverge on Pampeluna. Thus acting against the extremities, every advance he should make would oblige the other defensive corps to fall back, which would affect the resistance of his immediate opponent, and it would require only one advantage of combat or manœuvre, in a distance of thirty miles, to force one of the defensive corps from the road of Pampeluna, on which his own forces would be certain to unite.

Early on the morning of the 25th of July, the Count D'Erlon, with 13,000 men, made an attack on the position of Maya, advancing against the right, where the ridges of the mountains branched off towards his camp. The force on the position was not sufficient to resist such numbers, and the allies were driven back some miles, with the loss of 1,600 in killed and wounded. Arriving on a strong piece of ground where Sir R. Hill was enabled to concentrate all the troops under his command, the French desisted from further offensive movements.

Marshal Soult in person with 35,000 men advanced against Ronscevalles. General Byng commanded the advance of the allies in the pass, and being aware that a few miles to his right a road through Arbaceite turned his post, he detached Morillo's corps as far to the right as was consistent with mutual support, and placed his own brigade in a situation to cover the direct communication from St. Jean Pied de Port to that

P

town. After some skirmishing with a part of General Cole's division Soult directed his main effort against the front of General Byng's force, and drove it to the top of the mountain, which uncovered the road to Arbai-cete.   The same evening the Spanish regiments defending that town were successfully attacked and driven back on General Cole's division, who, having a superior force in his front, and on his flank, with the chance of one also getting in his rear, retired as soon it became dark to Lizoain, where the troops from Alduides joined him through Egue.   In conse-quence of this retrograde movement, Sir Rowland Hill's corps fell back be-hind Irueta, where it took up an almost unattackable position.   On the 26th General Picton's division was engaged with the enemy, whose superiority of force, however, compelled him to fall back.   On the 27th Lord Wellington himself arrived, and victory, from that moment, was no longer doubtful.   As he rode past the different corps, he directed at once, with a sort of prophetic certainty, the positions which it would be best for each to take up. His presence re-animated the drooping spirits of the men, who had found themselves every day retrograding before the enemy.   Soult, on this day, had directed a furious attack to be made upon a hill on the right of the 4th division.   The importance of the post caused it to be vigorously defended during that and the following day, when the assailants were finally repulsed.

On the 28th the 6th division, under General Packenham, arrived, and had no sooner taken its position than it was attacked by a large body of the enemy, who were driven back with great loss.   The battle then be-came general along the front of the heights occupied by the 4th division, every regiment of which charged with the bayonet, some of them four dif-ferent times, and the result was a repulse of the enemy with immense slaughter.   On the 29th and 30th various operations were carried on. On the latter day Lord Wellington directed an attack upon the enemy, the success of which obliged them to abandon a position, described by his lordship as one " of the strongest, and most difficult of access that he had yet seen occupied by troops."   In their retreat from it they lost a great number of prisoners.   A separate attack on Sir Rowland Hill's position was also repelled after a hard contest ; and on the night of the 1st August the allied army occupied nearly the same ground as it did on the 25th July.

The extraordinary gallantry and perseverance displayed by the officers and men during these reiterated conflicts surpassed, perhaps, in all the essentials of military skill and personal bravery, all the exploits, great as they were, that had been achieved during the war.

On the 2d of August the enemy remained posted with two divisions on the Puerto de Echalar, and nearly their whole army was concentrated behind the Puerto. Lord Wellington determined to dislodge them by a combined movement of three advanced divisions. One of these, however, the 7th, under the command of Major General Barnes, being first formed, commenced the attack by itself, and actually drove the two divisions of the enemy from the formidable heights which they occupied. Lord Wellington, describing this brilliant achievement, said, " it is impossible I can extol too highly the conduct of Major General Barnes, and of those brave troops, which was the admiration of all who were witnesses of it." Private accounts stated, that in this gallant enterprize General Barnes had at least, twenty shots through his clothes and hat, and yet most miraculously escaped unhurt.

This part of the Spanish frontier was now entirely cleared of the enemy, and their loss in these conflicts was supposed to be not less than 15,000, of whom 4000 were prisoners. The loss of the allies was also considerable, though scarcely equal to what might have been expected from the severe actions in which they were successively engaged.

DESCRIPTION OF THE MEDAL.

OBVERSE.—Head of the Duke of Wellington.

REVERSE.—An allegorical representation of the British driving the French across the Pyrenees into France. The French Eagle is retreating before the British Lion, who had dispossessed the former of the *fulmen*, or power possessed on the South side of the Pyrenean mountains. Round the face of the Medal is this legend—" THE ENGLISH ARMY PASS THE PYRENEES." On the exergue, " 1813."

No. XXIV.

LORD LYNEDOCH.

THIS officer distinguished himself very early in the first war with revolutionary France. In the year 1793 he went up the Mediterranean with Lord Hood's fleet, landed with the troops at Toulon, and served as a volunteer and extra aide-de-camp to Lord Mulgrave. His conduct on that occasion obtained him much notice. It has been said that he took to the military profession, in order, if possible, to divert his mind from the severe grief he felt at the death of his lady, which took place in the year 1792. She was the daughter of Lord Cathcart, and sister to the Countess of Mansfield.

Thomas Graham, Baron Lynedoch of Balgowan, in the county of Perth, G. C. B. and K. T. S. is descended from the Grames of Scotland, and traces his ancestry to the royal blood of that country. His mother was Christian, fourth daughter of Charles Earl of Hopetown, who married Thomas Graham, esq. in April 1743. The present Lord Lynedoch was the only issue of that marriage, and he himself has no children.

When he returned to this country, after the siege of Toulon, he raised the 1st battalion of the 90th regiment, of which his commission as lieutenant-colonel commandant was dated Feb. 10, 1794. It was soon afterwards ordered to Gibraltar, but garrison duty not suiting the ardent wishes of Colonel Graham, he obtained permission to join the Austrian army, where he continued during the memorable summer of 1796. He was subsequently attached to the Austrian army in Italy, and was shut up in Mantua with General Wurmsur during the investment of that city.

Early in the year 1797 he returned to his native country, and in the autumn rejoined his regiment at Gibraltar, from whence he proceeded to the attack of Minorca with the late Sir Charles Stuart, where he greatly distinguished himself. He soon after besieged the island of Malta, having obtained the local rank of brigadier-general. He had under his command

the 30th and 89th regiments, and some corps embodied under his immediate direction. With this force he appeared before Malta in the month
of September 1798; but the French garrison held out till September 1800,
when, after a siege, or, more properly speaking, a blockade, of two years,
it surrendered. General Pigott having arrived a short time previously to
its capitulation, he had the honour of transmitting the account of the success which had attended the British arms.

He again returned to England, where he learned that his own regiment, the 90th, had covered itself with glory on the plains of Egypt.
Eager to partake of its dangers and its fame, he hastened to join it, but
when he landed in Egypt that country was completely conquered. He soon
quitted it, therefore, and travelled through Turkey, with Mr. Hutchinson,
the brother of Lord Hutchinson. He made some stay at Constantinople;
and peace being concluded, he resided a short time at Paris.

From 1803 to 1805 he served in Ireland with his regiment, but in the
latter year it was ordered to the West Indies, and he remained without active employment till the spring of 1808, when he solicited and obtained
permission to accompany Sir John Moore to Sweden. The expedition
proceeded to Gottenburgh, where the troops continued on board the
transports, while Sir John was endeavouring to make arrangements with
the court of Sweden. A misunderstanding, however, having arisen with
Gustavus, the mission was put an end to, and Sir John Moore was immediately ordered to proceed to Spain, whither he was accompanied by Colonel
Graham, who served during the whole of the campaign of 1808. On his
return to England he was promoted to the rank of Major General, and
afterwards commanded a division in the expedition to Walcheren, where he
was actively employed at the siege of Flushing.

In February 1811 he embarked for Cadiz, with the brevet rank of Lieutenant General. The possession of that town was obstinately disputed by
the Spanish patriots and French, and General Graham was sent to take
the command of the British troops in the fortress. On the 5th of March
he fought the battle of Barossa, which was one of the most gallant conflicts
that occurred during the peninsular war. He afterwards joined the army
of Lord Wellington, of which he was appointed second in command. He
was present at the siege of Ciudad Rodrigo, but having a complaint in his

eyes, he was obliged to return to England. Early in 1813, however, he again embarked for Spain, but was not engaged in any action of magnitude till the battle of Vittoria, when he commanded the left wing of the British army.

The next conspicuous service upon which Sir Thomas Graham was employed, was the reduction of the town and citadel of San Sebastian. Ten thousand men were placed under his command for this purpose. The town stands at the foot of a promontory washed by the sea, the approach being over a low sandy isthmus, occupied by one front of a fortification, on the left flank of which, at six or seven hundred yards distance, are considerable sand-hills. These completely enfilade, and take in reverse its front defences. To abridge the labour of the siege, it was determined to limit the operations to raising batteries on the sand-hills, from which to force a breach in the exposed wall, and as soon as this was practicable, to storm it, and trust to the quick movement of the assaulting columns to pass through the fire of the front line of works. Batteries were accordingly thrown up on the sand-hills; and on the 25th July 1813, two breaches being practicable, one thirty yards in front, the other ten, they were assaulted at the hour of low water. The storming party (amounting to about 2000 men) being ready, a mine which had been formed under the glacis of the front line of works was sprung as the signal to rush forward. This unexpected explosion created so much alarm among the garrison, that the advance reached the breach with little loss; but, on attempting to ascend it, so much fire was brought upon them from the front, and from different flanks which had not been silenced, that in a short time 500 men were killed and wounded, and the remainder returned into the trenches.

The siege was now converted into a blockade, nor were active operations resumed till after the decisive successes which were obtained over the enemy in the series of battles in the Pyrenees. It was then determined to renew the attack with an increased power of artillery, and by batteries to be established on the isthmus, which would continue the breach round the angle of the land front. Eighty pieces of ordnance, accordingly, on the 28th of August opened a direct fire, and when the breaches appeared nearly in a state to be assaulted, a proportion was turned against the defences, which, in a few hours, nearly subdued the fire of the place.

A little before noon, on the 31st of August the columns advanced to the assault. On their approach, the enemy exploded two mines, which blew down a wall under which the assailants were passing. Luckily, however, our troops were not in very close order, and only a few therefore were buried in the ruins. The remainder reached their point of attack, and many desperate efforts were made to carry the breach. It was indeed a most murderous assault, and scarcely inferior to the dreadful one of Badajos. Each time, on attaining the summit, a heavy and close fire from the entrenched ruins, within, destroyed all who attempted to remain, and those at the foot fell in great numbers from the flank fire. To supply this slaughter, fresh troops were sent forward, who advanced with intrepid alacrity, as fast as they could file out of the trenches, and a battalion of Portuguese gallantly forded the Urumea in face of the enemy's works.

Two hours of continued exertion had passed away, and the troops were yet on the face of the breach falling in great numbers, without being able to establish themselves on its summit. At length, a quantity of combustibles exploded within — the firmness of the defenders was shaken — the ardour of the assailants rose in proportion — and they redoubled their efforts to ascend. Success smiled upon their heroical firmness. The most advanced works were successively abandoned by the garrison, and at last the entrenchment behind the breach. The troops immediately pushed up in great numbers, assisted each other over the ruins, and descended into the town. Every attempt to check them behind various interior defences was in a moment overcome, and the garrison were driven into the castle.

On the 9th of September heavy batteries of mortars opened upon this last retreat, which did not long resist. After enduring the bombardment for two hours, the garrison, reduced to 1,300 effective, with 500 sick and wounded, surrendered prisoners of war. The casualties of the besiegers, in the two attacks, rather exceeded 3,700.

This was not the last exploit of Sir Thomas Graham in the Peninsular campaigns. The left of the British army being directed to pass the Bidassoa river, he was entrusted with that service, and on the 7th of October, after an obstinate resistance from the enemy, he succeeded in establishing the British army on French ground. Then he was satisfied; and yielding to the ill state of health, he resigned his command to Lieutenant General Sir John Hope, and returned to England.

On the 3rd of May 1814, after receiving the thanks of Parliament for his conduct in the Peninsula, he was raised to the peerage, by the title which we have already recited, with an annuity of £.2,000 per annum, to be enjoyed by the next two possessors of it.

DESCRIPTION OF THE MEDAL.

OBVERSE.—Head of his Lordship, modelled by Rouw, and engraved by Webb.

REVERSE.—Capture of the town of St. Sebastian. The naval and military objects here, shew the union of the two forces in its capture. The graceful and animated figure with a Sword in one hand and a Victor's Crown in the other, and mounted advancingly on the ramparts, explicitly shew the mode in which the place was taken by storm.

Pl. 7.

XXV

XXVI

XXVII

XXVIII

Normand sc.

London, Pub. July 1st 1820, by Henry Colburn & Co. Conduit Street.

No. XXV.

SURRENDER OF PAMPELUNA.

THE capture of this fortress, which took place on the 31st of October 1813, was the concluding event of the war in the west of Spain. Wellington was then hovering on the south-western frontiers of France, which he soon afterwards penetrated, having marched triumphantly from the borders of Portugal, after opening the campaign, without once retrograding.

Pampeluna is a remarkably strong fortress, and the capital of Navarre. The siege of it was entrusted to Don Carlos D'Espana, who conducted it with great skill and ability. The garrison made proposals of capitulation on the 26th of October, but upon conditions to which Don Carlos could not listen; and on the 31st they were compelled to surrender, on the indispensible terms of being made prisoners of war, and sent to England. During the siege of this place, which commenced in August, the sorties of the garrison had always been repulsed with loss, and the conduct of the Spanish Commander and his troops frequently received the highest praise from Lord Wellington. The final success of the operations carried on by Don Carlos D'Espana, was of great importance to the meditated movements of the British army, as it relieved its right wing from the service of covering the blockade.

DESCRIPTION OF THE MEDAL.

OBVERSE.—Head of the Duke of Wellington.

REVERSE.—The surrender of Pampeluna to the English, is described by a female with a turreted head (the ancient emblem of a fortified town), presenting her keys to a warrior on horseback. The legend—" ENGLAND PROTECTS THE TOWN OF POMPEII (the ancient name of Pampeluna)." On the exergue—" CAPITULATION OF PAMPELUNA, OCTOBER 31st, 1812."

In the personified figure of Pampeluna, there is a very appropriate character of eager surrender, expressive of admiration and gratitude to her British deliverer.

No. XXVI.

BATTLE OF TOULOUSE.

THE victory which Wellington gained at Toulouse over the French army, commanded by Marshal Soult, is the only one of which it can be said, it were better it had never been won. It was, in fact, a useless effusion of human blood, occasioned by the perfidy of the general to whom he was opposed. There is no longer a doubt that Soult knew of the capture of Paris by the Allies, and the abdication of Buonaparte, when he fought this battle. Perhaps he wished, if possible, to achieve one triumph over his great adversary before the war closed, and if so worthless an ambition was really his motive for sacrificing so many brave lives, it is some consolation to reflect how utterly his hopes were baffled.

It was on the 28th of March that Soult retired into Toulouse, pursued by the forces under Lord Wellington, and he immediately began to fortify it in such a way as he thought most likely to repel his victorious followers. That city presented many peculiar local advantages in furtherance of his design, being surrounded by a defensible wall, three fourths of which is covered by the *Canal Royal du Midi*, or by the Garonne, an impassable obstacle. All direct approach to the remaining fourth of the *enceinte* not covered by the rivers, was interdicted by the state of the cross roads, besides being flanked by a range of bold hills which lie to the eastward of the town, just beyond the canal. The French strongly occupied the summit of these heights with five redoubts, and formed various lines of entrenchment in support of them.

The heavy rains which came on about this period compelled Lord Wellington to halt for some days, and it was not until the 10th of April that his whole army was enabled to cross the river, and move towards the town.

The arrangements for the attack were, Sir Rowland Hill's corps to confine the enemy within his works on the left of the Garonne; Baron

Alten's light, and General Picton's third division to make a shew of attack, and prevent the enemy coming out by the road of Paris ; while Freire's Spaniards, and Sir Lowry Cole's and Sir Henry Clinton's divisions under Sir W. Beresford should attack the entrenched heights. The cavalry were to keep a look out above the town, to prevent any movement of the French cavalry.

Sir W. Beresford crossed the Ers, and formed his corps in three columns of lines in the village of Croix d'Orade, the 4th division leading, with which he immediately carried Montblanc. He then moved up the Ers in the same order, over most difficult ground, in a direction parallel to the enemy's fortified position ; and as soon as he reached the point at which he turned it, he formed his lines, and moved to the attack Lieutenant General Don Freire advanced to the front of the Croix D'Orade, where he formed his corps in two lines, with a reserve on the height in front of the left of the enemy's position, on which height the Portuguese artillery was placed, with Major General Ponsonby's brigade of cavalry of reserve, in the rear.

As soon as formed, and when it was seen Sir W. Beresford was ready, General Friere moved forward to the attack, in good order, though exposed to an exceedingly severe cannonade. The effects of this made them advance at too quick a rate. The stoutest and best runners greatly preceded their less active brethren, and before the first line arrived at a hollow road fifty yards from the enemy's entrenchments, it was completely broken. The reserve, perceiving this, fell into the opposite extreme, and moved forward so slowly as not to be near enough to lend support. The French vigorously advanced upon the Spaniards, who had taken shelter under the bank, drove them down the hill, and would have siezed the bridge over the Ers, insulating the two divisions on the right, had they not been checked by a part of Baron Alten's light division. Sir T. Picton, who saw the great advantage to be gained by pushing across the canal, advanced against the work which defended the bridge on the left. When on the counterscarp the assailants discovered the formidable nature of its ditch, which rendered an assault impracticable, and brought them to a stand. Meanwhile, a heavy fire of musketry from within the line was fast thinning their front, and a numerous artillery was playing on their flank. There was no shelter of any kind near at hand, and a speedy retreat alone saved them from annihilation.

The enemy still held his entrenchment and four of the redoubts, and an interval for arrangement was given him, while the Spaniards were reforming, and General Beresford bringing up his artillery, which had been placed in battery in front of the village of Montblanc, to cannonade the works on the heights. These objects being accomplished, Sir H. Clinton advanced against one of the redoubts, which being incomplete, the enemy abandoned it, but immediately afterwards employed an entire division to retake it. A British battalion placed in the interior fought most gallantly. They were, however, nearly exhausted, when a brigade came to their assistance, which, charging the assailants, drove them down the hill. The French immediately formed a still more powerful body behind the canal for a second attempt, on which the defenders of the work, having been reinforced, planted their colours on the parapet in proud defiance of the threatened effort.

The French fought with a courage worthy of their best days. The equal and unvarying firmness of their opponents, however, prevailed, and they could not be dislodged from the work, though it was surrounded by such numbers of the enemy that no one could shew his head above the parapet. They at length relinquished the attempt, and retired behind the canal. The garrison of the remaining works, witnessing this failure, and seeing Sir Henry Clinton's division advancing from the right, as well as the Spaniards from the left, they feared to risk the assault, and evacuated their posts. The object of the attack was thus accomplished, and the allies formed on the hills, which look down into the city. At night, every post of the French retired within their defensive line behind the canal; and the allies had possession of the only bridge remaining over the Ers. The *debouché* from that over the Garonne, was too closely and too strongly guarded by Sir R. Hill to be forced.

The army being thus established on the three sides of Toulouse, Lord Wellington immediately detached the light cavalry to cut off the communication by the only road, practicable for carriages, which remained to the enemy. Thus, after a succession of masterly movements, Soult was driven into a situation of inextricable difficulty. He had, however, at his disposal 35,000 troops, and desperation might have given a force to his expiring efforts, which would have occasioned a severe loss to the brave men who held him encaged. The conclusion of peace, also, though not officially known to Lord Wellington, was too credibly reported to be doubted. Desirous, therefore, of avoiding a further effusion of blood, he permitted the French army without molestation to file out of the town, on the night of the 12th, by the road of Carcassone, passing within cannon shot under the heights of Pagada, crowned by his troops and bristling with his artillery.

As the operations of the day consisted entirely in the attack of formidable entrenchments, the loss of the victors was very considerable. Above 4,500 British and Portuguese were killed or wounded, and more than half that number of Spaniards. The loss of the enemy was also severe. They left in the hands of the allies Generals D'Harispe, Burrot, and St. Hilaire, and 1,600 prisoners. One piece of cannon was taken on the field of battle, and others, and large quantities of stores of all descriptions in the town.

On the 13th messengers arrived at Toulouse to announce the entry of the allies into Paris, the abdication of Buonaparte, and the restoration of the Bourbons. A convention for the suspension of hostilities, and for arranging a line of demarcation between the respective armies followed on the 18th April. Soon after, the Portuguese and Spaniards recrossed the Pyrenees, and the British marched to Bordeaux to embark.

DESCRIPTION OF THE MEDAL.

OBVERSE.—Head of Britannia, with a helmet, crowned with laurel, and embossed with the national emblem of her power, a Lion.

REVERSE.—The establishment of the Bourbons on the French Throne, by the defeat of the French forces at Toulouse, is well expressed by the figure of Wellington planting a white and lilied standard with one hand, and holding a laurel wreath and a palm with the other, as it rests on a trophy of French military articles, with the words " BATTLE OF TOULOUSE;" the date of it on the exergue, " 10TH APRIL, 1814."

This reverse is very explanatory of the defeat and first overthrow of Napoleon, as it was the last battle victoriously fought by the British previously to the first establishment of Louis on the French Throne.

No. XXVII.

THE PEACE OF EUROPE.

THE history of the world furnishes no example of such a stupendous change as was wrought in the political aspect of Europe, within the short space of two years. When Buonaparte projected and executed his invasion of Russia, when he marched a countless army to the banks of the Borysthenes, while his legions were also fighting on the shores of the Tagus, who would have been bold enough to predict the approaching destruction of his colossal power? Yet, the crisis of his fate was at hand. His star of glory, which rose at Lodi, and had so long dazzled the nations of Europe with its flaming lustre, turned pale at Moscow, where a sublime act of patriotism left him master of only a heap of smoking ruins. He fled to Paris, and was the first who told the portentous tidings. He was followed by the indignant armies of Russia and Prussia, and he knew that the other continental states who still appeared on his side waited but an auspicious moment to imitate the example of those two powers. That moment soon came. The bloody day of Leipsic, so fatal to Napoleon, so glorious for Europe, rallied round the standard of freedom myriads of troops, who, goaded by the deep sense of long and multiplied sufferings, beleagured the confines of that France, whose vanquished Emperor had so often repelled with scorn the possibility of invasion. She was invaded, not only on the East, and the North, but in the South, by the victorious army of Wellington, who, indeed, anticipated the triumphs of Germany, and was the first that planted a hostile banner on " the sacred territory."

Buonaparte struggled fiercely to retain his falling sceptre. He disputed every inch of ground with his pursuers, and often balanced the scale of victory. At length, however, a masterly manœuvre placed the capital in the hands of the allies (March 31, 1814), and there no longer existed a possibility of retrieving his fortunes. Within the walls of Paris, his enemies dictated a peace which for ever excluded from the throne of France himself and his family.   The banished Bourbons were recalled, and Louis XVIII. resumed the sceptre of his ancestors.   Buonaparte was permitted to choose his future abode.   He selected the island of Elba, whither he retired, accompanied by the execrations of millions, while Europe rang with undissembled joy at the recovery of her liberty, and the restoration of UNIVERSAL PEACE.

DESCRIPTION OF THE MEDAL.

OBVERSE.—Head of Britannia.

REVERSE.—Hercules in an attitude of repose, standing on a Napoleon standard,—a strong and classical reference to the quiescent state of the European belligerents in general, and of England in particular, after the long and severe struggle with France.   The club in the grasp of Hercules is an apt designation of the attitude of preparation for sudden war, and for promptly repelling aggression.   Inscription, " THE REPOSE OF HERCULES, 1814."

No. XXVIII.

THE PRINCE REGENT.

THE inscription on the exergue of this Medal expresses an historical fact, which will dignify the character of England to the latest posterity. She did, indeed, " give peace to the world." It was her undaunted perseverance, her noble struggle, single-handed, with the mighty despotism of imperial France; her unparalleled sacrifices of blood and treasure; her proud, untameable defiance of the Gallic eagle, which finally achieved the peace of Europe.

Let it not be forgotten, however, that in the glory of the triumph, the Sovereign claims his share. Had his councils been less decisive,—had his purpose been less fixed,—had there been a particle of weakness, or hesitation in the royal mind, the country could not have signalized itself in the way it did. The REGENT, administering his high office, in trust for his venerable sire, anxiously endeavoured to tread in that path which he knew his father would have trodden, had he been permitted by Providence to direct the march of public events. Hence the unbending hostility which this country displayed towards the arrogant pretensions and insulting aggressions of Napoleon. Hence, too, the justice of that acknowledgment on the part of Louis XVIII. who, when he made his triumphal entry into London, after his recall to the French throne, observed to the Regent, " It is to your Royal Highness's councils, to this great country, and to the constancy of its people, that I shall always ascribe, under Providence, the restoration of our house to the throne of our ancestors." No one will deny this declaration ;—no one will deny, that the subversion of Napoleon's power, and the opportunity for the Bourbons to re-ascend the throne, were the results of that unshaken perseverance on the part of England, which no peril, no sacrifice, no temptation could relax or overcome. This intrepid example not only taught other nations how they might save themselves, but presented a bulwark and defence round which they might rally in the common cause whenever they had spirit and patriotism enough to rouse from their lethargy. Most emphatically, therefore, and most truly, may it be said, that " ENGLAND GAVE PEACE TO THE WORLD."

DESCRIPTION OF THE MEDAL.

OBVERSE.—Head of his Royal Highness, with the inscription, " GEORGE PRINCE REGENT, 1816."

REVERSE.—Britannia giving peace to mankind, described by her presentation of an olive-branch to the genius of the world, with the inscription, " ENGLAND GIVES PEACE TO THE WORLD, 1814."

No. XXIX.

TREATIES OF PARIS.

THE subjects commemorated by this medal are so similar to those upon which we have expatiated in the two preceding ones, that it would be mere repetition to enlarge upon them again. When Buonaparte escaped from Elba, and reinstated himself in his former power, he found England the same invincible obstacle to his ambition, as she had proved herself throughout his whole career. The immediate results of that transaction will more appropriately be traced in some of the subsequent medals, (Nos. 35, 36, 37, and 38.) and to them we refer the reader.

DESCRIPTION OF THE MEDAL.

OBVERSE.—Bust of the Prince Regent.

REVERSE.—The hope of Europe, that the long and devastating war might be crowned with peace, is here allegorically represented by a figure of Peace, with wings at rest, reclining on an anchor amidst trophies of war conquered from France, among which is the significant emblem of the annihilated power of Buonaparte—a broken Eagle. In her hand is a serpent, the type of Wisdom, and suitable to that direction of affairs which, in union with physical power, obtained the result of peace. On a pedestal supporting the figure is inscribed " TREATIES OF PARIS." On the exergue " 30TH MAY, 1814 ; 20TH NOVEMBER, 1815." Above is the inscription, " ARMIS ET CONSILIIS," an inscription well appropriated to the power and the counsels which achieved the great result of peace.

XXIX

XXX

XXXI

XXXII

London Pub. July 1.st 1820, by Henry Colburn & C.º Conduit Street.

No. XXX.

VISIT OF THE ALLIED SOVEREIGNS TO ENGLAND.

ON the 6th of June 1814, the Emperor of Russia, and the King of Prussia, with his two sons and their respective suites, including many of their most distinguished generals, Marshal Blucher, General Von Yorck, General Bulow, the Hetman Platoff, Count Barclay de Tolly, &c. &c. embarked at Boulogne, on board the Impregnable, the flag ship of the Duke of Clarence, by whom they were landed the same evening at Dover. Early in the afternoon of the following day, the two Sovereigns reached London in the most private manner. The Emperor took up his residence with his sister, the Duchess of Oldenburg, at the Pulteney Hotel in Piccadilly, and the King of Prussia at Clarence House. On the 8th the former held a levee, at the apartments of the Duke of Cumberland, prepared for his reception, and which was attended by the Prince Regent, the Duke of York, and a great number of persons of distinction. The King of Prussia also held a levee which was similarly attended; and in the evening, Her Majesty held a court at her palace, for the purpose of receiving the illustrious strangers.

On the 9th a grand court was held at Carlton House, and afterwards a chapter of the Order of the Garter, when the King of Prussia, the Earl of Liverpool, and Viscount Castlereagh, were admitted Knights of the Order. The following day the Monarchs repaired to Ascot Heath to witness the races, which were also attended by Her Majesty, the Prince Regent, and the Princesses. They afterwards partook of an entertainment provided for them by the Queen at Frogmore. To describe, however, all their movements, the places they visited, the crowds that followed their footsteps, and the general hilarity which pervaded the metropolis, would be foreign to the purpose of this work. It shall only, therefore, be further observed, that they visited Oxford, and the Royal Arsenal at Woolwich, and that on the 18th they went in state to Guildhall, to partake of a magnificent entertainment prepared for them by the City of London.   The grandeur of this banquet surpassed all description. On the 22nd they proceeded to Portsmouth, accompanied by His Royal Highness the Prince Regent, where, after enjoying the novel spectacle of a naval review, they embarked for the Continent.   It would be impossible to describe the enthusiastic eagerness of all classes to obtain a sight of the illustrious strangers, or the unbounded demonstrations of joy with which they were every where received.   The Emperor Alexander, in particular, by his easy familiarity and frank condescension, was extremely popular during his short abode.   The King of Prussia, habitually reserved, and, it is said, his mind oppressed with melancholy reflections on the disasters to which his family had been exposed by the ferocious tyranny of Buonaparte, attracted much less of public attention.

DESCRIPTION OF THE MEDAL WHICH RECORD THIS EVENT.

OBVERSE.—Head of Britannia, classically exemplifying her power by the Helmet and the noble animal upon it.

REVERSE.—The visits of the Sovereigns of Russia and Prussia to England is here told, by the arrival of the foreign ship on its shores, where Neptune holds his chief sway.   The universal peace which has been just conquered by the Allies from France, is exemplified by the Temple of Janus, and its closed doors.

No. XXXI.

DUKE OF CAMBRIDGE.

WHEN the liberation of Germany took place, after the sanguinary and gigantic conflict at Leipsic, the Hanoverian dominions of His Majesty, which had been seized by Buonaparte in 1803, reverted to their former connexion with the crown of Great Britain. The immediate instrument of their deliverance from the yoke of France, was the Crown Prince of Sweden, who after the battle of Leipsic, marched with his army northwards, and on the 6th November 1813 moved his head quarters from Gottingen, where he arrived on the 31st October, to Hanover. His entry was preceded by a proclamation (November 4th) addressed to the Hanoverians, by the two Privy Counsellors Decken and Bremer, announcing the resumption of the government of the Electoral dominions.

In 1814 His Royal Highness the Duke of Cambridge was appointed Governor General of the Kingdom of Hanover; for to that rank, as a continental state, it had been elevated by His Royal Highness the Prince Regent. On the 24th of October 1814, Count Munster, the Hanoverian Minister of State, delivered a note to the Austrian Minister, and to the Ministers of the other powers assembled at the Congress at Vienna, announcing this change in the royal title of Hanover. In this note, the Prince Regent observed, that the title of Electoral Prince of the Holy Roman Empire was no longer suitable to the actual circumstances of the Germanic States; that several of the principal powers of Germany had, in consequence, invited him to renounce that title, as it would be the means, among other things, of facilitating many of the arrangements which the future welfare of Germany seemed to require; and that therefore, His Royal Highness had resolved, laying aside in the name of his House the Electoral title, to declare that he erected his provinces forming the country of Hanover, into a kingdom, and that he should henceforth assume the title of King of Hanover.

A proclamation was subsequently issued to the Hanoverians (October 26th), declaring this change, and commanding that in future in all acts, &c. instead of the old titles, they should employ that of " King of the United Kingdoms of Great Britain and Ireland, King of Hanover, Duke of Brunswick and Lunenberg, &c."

Hanover received some extension of its territories at the Congress of Vienna.

His Royal Highness the Duke of Cambridge has continued, since 1814, in the function of Governor General, and by the wisdom of his political conduct, as well as the amiable influence of his personal character, has conciliated the loyalty and affection of the inhabitants.

DESCRIPTION OF THE MEDAL.

OBVERSE.—His Royal Highness the Duke of Cambridge.

REVERSE.—Entry of the English into Hanover, which is here allegorized by Britannia giving succour to the Hanoverian Horses.

No. XXXII.

FLIGHT OF NAPOLEON FROM ELBA.

IT is impossible to deny, that when the allies, after the capture of Paris in 1814, permitted Buonaparte to select Elba as his place of residence, with a guard consisting of his most devoted soldiers, and so near the theatre of his former exploits, they at least assembled together the elements of that explosion which afterwards took place. It is not, however, clear that this hazardous experiment could be avoided. When Buonaparte signed his abdication, the state of France was by no means such as to render the further operations of the allied armies a matter of certain success. Buonaparte, too, had a considerable army with him, and he might have augmented that force by other corps which were scattered over different parts of France. Under such circumstances, it was, perhaps, the only policy they could safely pursue, not to impose too rigorous conditions upon the fallen ruler. It is probable, also, they might contemplate some future opportunity of removing him to a less accessible abode. Among the many motives, indeed, which have been imputed to Buonaparte for returning to France, at the time he did, was his alleged knowledge of such an intention on the part of the allies. Although this accusation has never been proved, it is not devoid of probability. The allies could not dictate his place of retreat at Fontainbleau; but they might deem it expedient to alter it at Vienna. At Fontainbleau he was still a Sovereign and negotiated as one; at Elba he had the name without the power, and must have acquiesced in conditions which he could not dispute.

We pass, however, from the motives of his enterprize, to the enterprize itself. When he had finally determined upon the attempt to recover his imperial crown, he did not suffer a single hour to elapse unprofitably. He concealed his project, till the moment of executing it, so entirely, that even General Bertrand was unacquainted with it the very

evening before.   On the 25th of February he gave an entertainment to
his little court, and during the evening he appeared more than ordinarily
tranquil and affable.   On the 26th he reviewed his troops, and at one
o'clock they received orders to prepare for their departure.   But whither?
No one could tell.   Was it to France or Italy?   A few hours dispelled
the mystery, and every heart beat with exultation, as every tongue pronounced, with enthusiasm, *Paris, or death!*   By four o'clock, they were
all on board, Napoleon and his officers being the last who quitted the
island.   The fleet which was employed to convey this band of desperate
adventurers, with their sanguine leader, to the shores of France, consisted of only seven small vessels, one of which was a brig, (L'Incon-
stant) mounting twenty-six guns.   The number of troops has been stated
at eleven hundred and forty; viz. 400 of the old guard; 200 infantry;
1,000 of the Polish Light Horse; and 200 of the *bataillon des flanqueurs.*
The remainder was composed of Corsicans and Elbeans.

On the 1st of March, at three o'clock in the afternoon, the restless
chieftain and his band entered the gulf of San Juan, a short distance from
Frejus, in the department of the Var.   Previously to disembarking his
troops, Buonaparte summoned them all into his presence, and addressing
them in a brief but energetic speech, ordered that they should cast the
cockade of Elba into the sea, and assume the tri-coloured one.   That
badge he distributed with his own hands, and it was received by the soldiers with loud and enthusiastic shouts of *Vive l'Empereur!*

When his soldiers were all landed, he himself followed, and as his foot
once more touched the soil of France, he exclaimed with exultation,
Voila la Congres dissous!   It *was* dissolved, but it was only in its political functions or capacity.   The members composing that august body,
animated by one common feeling of interest and indignation, united themselves still more closely for warlike purposes, and rushed to arms for the
independence and honour of Europe.

It belongs not to this work to trace the invader, step by step, till he
once more entered Paris, and resumed his abdicated throne.   It was the
treachery of the army which opened for him an unobstructed path to the
Tuilleries.   Along the whole line of his march, they received him with
acclamations.   They were tainted with disloyalty throughout their entire

mass. No part was whole ; no part was sound. Napoleon had only to hear that a corps was marching against him, to know that it was so many men added to his force. So perfectly, indeed, was this comprehended by his partisans, that a few days before the departure of Louis from Paris, the following sarcasm appeared on one of the gates of the Tuilleries : " The Emperor requests the king not to send him any more soldiers, as he has enough already." Such being the case, it may rather excite surprise, that he did not sooner reach the capital, than that he reached it when he did.

It was on the evening of the 11th of March that a messenger, despatched from Paris, conveyed to the Congress at Vienna the portentous tidings of Napoleon's entry into France. The ministers of the different allied powers immediately assembled, and on the 13th of March was issued that celebrated declaration, in which it was insisted, that by quitting Elba, and re-appearing in France, with projects of rebellion and treason, he had placed himself beyond the protection of the laws, and manifested to the world that he was a being with whom neither truce nor peace could be concluded. They therefore declared that he had placed himself out of the pale of civil and social relations, and rendered himself liable to public vengeance. This declaration was signed by the respective ministers of Austria, Russia, France, England, Prussia, Spain, Portugal and Sweden.

Napoleon meanwhile pursued his march, and on the 20th of March, at nine in the evening, he entered Paris, but so privately, that it was scarcely known he had arrived, except to those of his own party who had made preparations to receive him. Louis XVIII. had quitted the capital the preceding night.

DESCRIPTION OF THE MEDAL.

OBVERSE.—The Flight of Napoleon from Elba is here emblematically expressed by an Eagle with a thunder-bolt, advancing to the French coast from the isle of Elba. The broken down doors of the temple of Janus shadow out

S

the rupture of the general Peace consequent on Buonaparte's flight. The date of this flight is on the exergue.

REVERSE.—Mercury (the fabled Messenger of the Gods) is carrying an account of the event throughout Europe, with an invitation, " To ARMS." On the face of the Medal is marked " DECLARATION OF THE CONGRESS OF VIENNA." On the exergue is the date of the Declaration " 13TH MARCH."

XXXIII

XXXIV

XXXV

 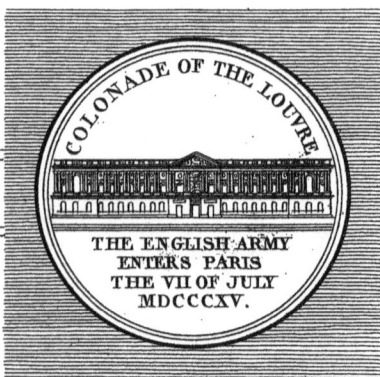

XXXVI

Normand filt

London. Pub. July 1st 1820. by Henry Colburn & Co. Conduit Street.

No. XXXIII.

THE BRITISH ARMY IN THE NETHERLANDS.

THE historical notice that would be necessary to accompany this Medal will be found more appropriately attached to No. XXXV. which commemorates the battle of Waterloo. That mighty conflict was the only transaction connected with the presence of our army in the Netherlands in the year 1815 that is capable of descriptive illustration.

DESCRIPTION OF THE MEDAL.

OBVERSE.—The Bull, a noble but common animal of the Netherlands, together with the peculiar buildings (Brussels) in the back ground, denote the Low Countries, and the British Standard planted on its ground, the establishment and success of the British arms there in 1815.

REVERSE.—The river god of the Scheldt, on whose waters the British naval and military power is floating.

No. XXXIV.

THE MARQUIS OF ANGLESEY.

THIS gallant and distinguished nobleman was born on the 17th May 1768, and is the eldest son of the late Earl of Uxbridge, whom he succeeded in his titles and estate on the 13th of March 1812. At an early period of the revolutionary war with France, his lordship raised a regiment of infantry, with which, as lieutenant colonel, he served on the continent, under his Royal Highness the Duke of York. He afterwards exchanged into the cavalry, and being advanced to the rank of major general, he accompanied Sir John Moore in the memorable expedition to Spain, where he was highly distinguished for the spirit and bravery with which he led the cavalry brigade in several successful attacks upon the best troops of France. He afterwards served under the Duke of Wellington during nearly the whole of the peninsular war. When the peace of Europe was again disturbed by the unexpected escape of Buonaparte from the island of Elba, his Lordship promptly obeyed the call of his country, and forsaking all the enjoyments of his exalted station, betook himself to the tented field. In the tremendous conflict at Waterloo, where he rendered the most distinguished services, he received a wound which occasioned the amputation of his right leg. It was for the gallantry of his conduct in this battle that he was elevated to the dignity of a marquisate (on the 23d June 1815) by the title of Marquis of Anglesey.

It will be necessary, however, to detail the particulars of that brilliant charge, on the glorious 18th of June, which is commemorated by this Medal.

It was at the most critical moment of the battle that the Earl of Uxbridge led on the cavalry against the enemy. Sir Thomas Picton had fallen in a desperate struggle, and his division was nearly overpowered by superior numbers. The Earl of Uxbridge, who had watched the conflict, saw at length a favourable moment for operating. He galloped up to the second brigade ; and the regiments which composed it (1st, 2d, and 6th dragoons) wheeling into line, presented a beautiful front of about 1300 men. He was received with an enthusiastic cheer as he rode along; when, perceiving that our infantry was likely to be outflanked by the French, he led a charge which was most gallantly executed. They took the enemy in flank, and a tremendous cavalry fight commenced with the lancers and cuirassiers. The three regiments were typically representative of the British Empire,—the Royals, the Greys, and the Inniskillens. Every man fought with unparalleled heroism, for every man had his own individual part to perform. Neither the defensive armour of the cuirassiers, nor the deadly weapon of the lancers, could protect their owners from the resistless onset of this brigade. The slaughter was prodigious ; and the manner in which the Scots Greys plunged into the thickest of the fight, dealing destruction around them, excited equally the wonder and the apprehensions of Napoleon. " What fine troops !" he exclaimed ; " what a pity it is I shall cut them all to pieces !" Even our own officers trembled for the safety of those gallant and daring men, who frequently encountered masses of the enemy which trebled their own numbers.

Nor was this the only exploit of the cavalry, whom the noble Earl commanded, on that sanguinary day. It was the opinion of many that the battle was more than once restored by their timely operations. Towards its close, indeed, they committed dreadful havoc, and it was in the last of these resistless onsets that the Earl of Uxbridge received his wound, by almost the last shot that was fired.

DESCRIPTION OF THE MEDAL.

OBVERSE.—Head of the Marquis, round which is inscribed, " HENRY WILLIAM MARQUIS OF ANGLESEY ;" and on the bottom of the neck, the name of the engraver, Mr. Mills, with C. the initial of Chantry, the name of the unrivalled sculptor of the bust from which the Medal was engraved.

REVERSE.—The Marquis of Anglesey is leading his famous charge of cavalry against the French Imperial Guard. A French soldier in despair is, on the approach of the Marquis, breaking an Eagle. The inscription is, " CHARGE OF THE BRITISH AT WATERLOO."

No. XXXV.

THE BATTLE OF WATERLOO.

THE battle of Waterloo was one of those decisive and stupendous contests on which the destinies of mighty empires depend, and from whose single issue greater events devolve than are sometimes produced by a whole series of campaigns. The repose of Europe, which had been broken, from one end to the other, by the sudden landing of Buonaparte in France, was instantly restored by his defeat at Waterloo. Had he triumphed, instead of having been vanquished, who would have been bold enough to predict the consequences that might, and in all probability must have ensued.

This great battle was fought on the 18th of June 1815. We cannot attempt to narrate the political or military events that preceded it. They have already filled volumes, from the pens of various writers in England, in France, and in Germany. We must confine our description to a strict and brief account of the battle itself.

It was about five o'clock in the afternoon of the 17th that our army, after the conflict at Quatre Bras on the preceding day, and after a fatiguing march, reached the ground upon which they were, next morning, to sustain the mighty shock. The remainder of the evening was employed by the different divisions taking up their respective posts. The position which they occupied was the following.

In the extreme rear was the forest of Soignies, through which runs a paved road from Brussels to Charleroi. At a small distance from the entrance to this forest is the village of Waterloo, where the Duke of Wellington established his head quarters. The right of the army was thrown back to a ravine near Merke Braine, which was occupied, and its left extended to a height above the hamlet of Ter la Haye, which was also occupied. Along nearly the whole extent of our front was a gentle declivity, which formed, in most places, an admirable glacis. At the bottom of this declivity, immediately in front of our left centre, was the farm-house of La Haye Sainte, occupied by a detachment of Hanoverians. In front of the right centre, and near the Nivelles road, was the chateau of Hougomont, which covered the return of that flank. Here the guards were posted, with 300 Nassau troops, employed as sharp-shooters. The Duke of Wellington attached the greatest importance to this position, and during the battle sent repeated orders to maintain it.

The extreme right of the British army, turning rather backwards, extended as far as Merke Braine, to protect the Nivelles road, while an advanced corps occupied the village of Braine-le-Leud. From the immediate left of our line, in front of Ter la Haye, was a road leading to Ohain, and the woody passes of St. Lambert, by which the communication with the Prussians was maintained. A part of Lord Hill's corps, consisting of nearly the whole 4th division, under Lieutenant General Sir C. Colville, was stationed at Halle to protect Brussels in case the enemy should turn the right of the British, and march upon that city. Lord Hill himself commanded the reserve, in front of the village of Merke Braine, with its right resting on Braine-le-Leud.

The position occupied by the French was on a ridge parallel to the heights where the British were stationed. The distance between the two lines varied in breadth from one thousand to twelve hundred yards. This small extent added greatly to the slaughter, and particularly enabled the artillery to maintain a certain and destructive fire. The whole range from right to left was scarcely more than a mile and a half, while from the rear of the French to that of the British might be about two miles. Buonaparte established his head-quarters at the farm-house of Caillou, near Planchenoit, on the 17th; and on the 18th at La Belle Alliance.

Such were the positions of the two armies. Their numerical strength, according to the most accurate computations, is stated thus : the combined British army 60,000; the French army 100,000. To this may be added, 296 pieces of cannon, while the British and Belgian artillery did not exceed 150.

Towards noon, on the 18th, all the preliminary movements being completed, the battle began with a furious attack by Jerome's division, forming a part of the second corps, against Hougomont. This post, as already mentioned, was occupied by a detachment of the guards. The whole force did not exceed 1500 men, exclusively of the 300 Nassau troops, and was commanded, at first, by Lieutenant Colonel Macdonald, and afterwards by Lieutenant Colonel Home. Lieutenant Colonel Lord Saltoun commanded the light companies of the 1st guards, who were stationed in the wood which surrounded the house. Against this post, thus feebly garrisoned, the enemy directed their whole second corps, consisting of nearly 30,000 men; not, indeed, in one combined attack, but by successive reinforcements during the day. It was formed into three divisions. Jerome Buonaparte was soon driven back, for our men defended themselves with obstinacy as in a citadel, the loop-holes that had been made enabling them to fire securely. Though the Nassau troops were quickly repulsed, the enemy never succeeded in keeping possession of the wood. It was repeatedly attempted to cut off the communication between Hougomont and the rest of the army ; but, except a temporary success, when the cavalry charged our squares, and for a moment remained upon the ridge immediately in its rear, all their endeavours proved unavailing, and the garrison was regularly reinforced with men, and supplied with ammunition. Finding every effort fruitless, to carry it by the sword, they at length strove to dislodge their brave opponents by setting fire to the house. The shells striking an ancient beam, it was soon enveloped in flames, which penetrated to the chapel. It is melancholy to relate, that many of the wounded, French as well as British, perished in the conflagration; but the guards still remained in their entrenchment, while the devouring element was raging above their heads. After this the vehemence of the attack somewhat abated, but it was not discontinued till the French were routed in the evening. The loss sustained by the enemy in their reiterated attempts to carry this post was enormous, being estimated at about 10,000 in killed and wounded. General Foy's division alone lost 3000. Our loss was small in proportion to that of the French, but great in proportion to the whole amount employed. It is stated at nearly 1000.

The attack upon Hougomont was accompanied by a very heavy cannonade, from more than 200 pieces of artillery, upon our whole line, intended to support the repeated charges of cavalry and infantry. These charges were sometimes made by the cavalry alone, sometimes by the infantry, and sometimes by both together. Our men were drawn up in nearly solid squares, each being several files deep, and so posted as to afford mutual aid. Sufficient space was allowed between the squares to deploy into line, when occasion required, while a third square, receding somewhat from the rear of those that were parallel, presented a menacing front to the enemy's cavalry as often as they penetrated beyond them, being thus encountered by a triple fire. In this firm and compact order of battle, with the artillery playing upon the French columns as they advanced, and the cavalry in reserve, ready to rush forward whenever opportunities occurred, our gallant soldiers sustained the conflict for nearly twelve hours.

Napoleon's plan of attack seemed to comprise a double object. While the divisions of his second corps were employed in endeavouring to turn our right, the first corps used every effort to penetrate our left centre; a combined operation, which, had it been successful, would have surrounded one half of the British army. In support of this design the most desperate charges of infantry and cavalry were made, in such numbers, that, to use the words of General Alava, " it required all the skill of his Lordship to post his troops, and all the good qualities of the latter to resist them." It was in one of these charges that the lamented Picton fell.

The battle raged with great fury at La Haye Sainte, in front of our left centre. When it was resolved to defend this place, the walls were loop-holed for the infantry to fire through; but unfortunately the entrance to the house fronted the high road, which being in the very line of the enemy's fire, it became ultimately impossible to supply the troops with ammunition when the contest was hotly carried on in the immediate neighbourhood of it. Its defence was entrusted to Col. Baring with a detachment of the German Legion, amounting to about 300 men, subsequently reinforced by 200 more. The shattered and dilapidated state of the house after the battle, conspicuously evinced the furious efforts which the enemy made for its possession, and the desperate courage displayed in its defence. The door was perforated with innumerable shot-holes; the roof destroyed by shells and cannon-balls; there was scarcely the vestige of a window discernible; and the whole edifice exhibited a melancholy scene of ravage and desolation. Yet, when obtained, it afforded no advantage commen-

T

surate to the loss with which it had been purchased; for our artillery on the adjacent ridge, continued to pour down such a destructive and incessant fire, that Napoleon could make but little use of the conquest to promote his subsequent operations. This, however, was the single, the solitary success, which attended the enemy during the whole day. In every other part of the field his utmost advantages consisted in momentary impressions produced by his impetuous onsets of cavalry.

Three great attacks, each of them a battle in itself, were made, and made in vain; they were followed by many desperate charges, which Buonaparte was accustomed to find decisive, but which, when directed against British troops, only augmented the unavailing slaughter. Night was approaching, and every thing depended upon being able to subdue Wellington before the arrival of the Prussians. Their advanced columns, emerging from the wood of Fischermont, already began to disclose his perilous condition. Fresh masses of cavalry and infantry were now brought forward, under cover of a heavy cannonade, against our centre and towards our right. The left was only so much engaged as might prevent it from detaching reinforcements. This was about five o'clock. The battle, which gradually extended itself nearly along the whole line, lasted above an hour, when, after prodigious efforts, and a carnage horrible beyond description, the assailants were once more repulsed.

Napoleon must have witnessed this failure with no common feelings of dismay, for the operations of the Prussians upon his right flank and rear now began to assume a more serious character. Blucher had put his army in motion at day break, and about seven o'clock in the evening they arrived on the field of battle. This decided the issue. Blucher was manoeuvring to get into the rear of the French, but Buonaparte, not choosing to remain till the Prussians should be in force upon the high road to Genappe, and seeing his doom pronounced, uttered the memorable words, " We must save ourselves !" The Duke of Wellington, who instantly observed the confusion which manifested itself along the French line, exclaimed, " Now every man must advance." This decisive step, determined upon with that unerring sagacity by which he had so often controlled events, consummated the disasters of the enemy. The order was no sooner given than executed. The flying enemy were cut down unresistingly by their eager and exasperated pursuers. The slaughter was terrific, for, in their consternation they had thrown from them their arms, as incumbrances which only impeded escape; even the rout at Vittoria sunk in comparison with the ruin which now overtook the enemy. General Gneisenau described it as resembling the flight of a horde of barbarians, and said the road to Genappe presented the appearance of an immense shipwreck; it was covered with an innumerable quantity of cannon, caissons, carriages, baggage, arms, and wrecks of every kind. The pursuit was continued by the British and Prussians as far as Genappe, where the Duke of Wellington and Blucher met, and exchanged mutual congratulations upon the glorious issue of the battle. Finding himself on the same road with Blucher, and his troops being exhausted with fatigue, it was agreed that the Prussians, who were comparatively fresh, should continue to follow the enemy. Well did the veteran hero execute his task.

The loss we sustained was great, and could be compensated only by the mighty triumph which it purchased. The total of British and Hanoverians who were killed or wounded, amounted to at least 10,000; and the Belgians and Brunswickers were computed at one third as many. An unusual number of commanding officers were either killed or wounded, a melancholy proof of the ardour and intrepidity with which they discharged their duty.

The loss sustained by the French has never been exactly ascertained; but the most moderate estimate fixes it at 20,000 men left dead on the field of battle, besides 7,000 prisoners, 203 pieces of artillery, and the whole *materiel* of their army. Among the prisoners were Count Lobau, who commanded the 6th corps, and General Cambronne.

DESCRIPTION OF THE MEDAL.

OBVERSE.—Head of his Grace the Duke of Wellington, by Brenet.

REVERSE.—A broad wreath of laurel, among which is entwined the names of the principal victories obtained in the Peninsula and France. In the centre is inscribed the name of the final victory over Buonaparte, with its date; and above are joined hands, emblems of the meeting and co-operation upon that great event of the Allied Generals.

THE DUKE OF WELLINGTON.

THE battle of Waterloo was fought on the 18th of June 1815, and so rapid was the march of the allied troops under the command of the Duke of Wellington and Prince Blucher, that on the 3d of July following, Paris capitulated. By the eighth article of that capitulation, however, it was stipulated that all the barriers of that capital were not to be given up till the 6th. On that day, accordingly, they were occupied by the allied troops, and on the following morning, the 7th, the British army entered Paris as conquerors ! The conditions granted by the victors to the vanquished, were not only honourable to their spirit of moderation and forbearance, but remarkably contrasted with the penal and confiscating capitulations commonly forced upon their enemies by Napoleon and his generals.

The reverse of the Medal which commemorates this event, naturally brings to our recollection that celebrated letter, which the Duke of Wellington wrote to Lord Castlereagh, justifying the restoration of those plundered works of art which the Louvre contained. The policy of leaving those fruits of military rapacity untouched at the period of the first capture of Paris, was more than questionable. To have abstained from restoring these to their rightful owners after the second, would have been pusillanimous.

" The feelings of the people of France," observed the Duke of Wellington, upon this subject, must be founded on national vanity only. It must be a desire to retain these specimens of the arts, not because Paris is the fittest depository for them, but because they were obtained by military success, of which they are the trophies. The same feeling which induces the people of France to retain the pictures and statues of other nations, would naturally induce other nations to wish, now that success is on their side, that the property should be returned to its rightful owners."

This argument, thus simply and concisely stated, is a sufficient answer to the plausible sophistries which were employed in France, and in England too, against the restoration of these works of art. But it may be urged in addition, still using the language of the illustrious Duke, that " not only it would have been unjust in the Sovereigns to gratify the people of France at the expence of their own people; but the sacrifice they would make would be impolitic, as it would deprive them of the opportunity of giving to the people of France A GREAT MORAL LESSON." This lesson they were taught. May they profit by it hereafter !

DESCRIPTION OF THE MEDAL.

OBVERSE.—Head of his Grace, by Brenet.

REVERSE.--The Colonade of the Louvre is inscribed at top. The Colonade occupies the centre and diameter of the Medal. Below is inscribed, " THE ENGLISH ARMY ENTERS PARIS THE 7TH OF JULY, 1815." This is a faithful representation of the Louvre, an edifice very properly selected to record the entry of the British into Paris; as it was the great depository of the pictures and statues which Napoleon had obtained from the different countries he had conquered.

SURRENDER OF NAPOLEON.

No. XXXVIII.

NAPOLEON AT THE ISLAND OF ST. HELENA.

THE subjects of these two Medals are so intimately connected, that it will be better to blend the description of them. When Napoleon stepped on the quarter-deck of the Bellerophon, he placed himself in the hands of that power to whom the consent of Europe afterwards confided the permanent custody of his person; and his banishment to St. Helena was nothing more than the obvious consequence of his surrender.

When Buonaparte fled to Paris, after the disastrous field of Waterloo, he lingered there a few days in hopes there might be some demonstration on the part of the people of France in his favour, which would justify his attempting again to take the field against his enemies. In this, however, he was disappointed. Not only did the people remain passive, but the most zealous of his own partizans insisted upon the necessity of his again abdicating; or, in other words, that he should resign a power he was no longer able to maintain. Ever ready to follow those counsels which led to his own personal safety, he quitted Paris, with the intention of embarking for the United States of America, and arrived at Rochefort, a sea-port town, the 7th of July, 1815, the very day when the capital capitulated to the combined Prussian and English armies. Here he remained till the 8th, when he went on board the French frigate La Saale, and continued on board till the 14th. On the 10th the wind was favourable for putting to sea, but the English cruisers and moonlight nights made it too hazardous an experiment. On the 12th he learned from his brother Joseph, the dissolution of the Chambers, and the entrance of the King into Paris. Up to that moment he had constantly expressed an opinion, that the

XXXVII

XXXVIII

XXXIX

XL

Normand: fils.

London, Pub. July 1st 1820, by Henry Colburn & Co Conduit Street.

Chambers would recall him, but their being dissolved, and Louis XVIII. having resumed his throne, rendered that event no longer possible. Under these circumstances he had to choose one of three proceedings. He might remain at Rochefort, and be delivered as a prisoner into the hands of the allies : he might attempt to escape to America, and incur the almost certain consequence of being intercepted by the English ; or, he might at once surrender himself to the latter, and take his chance for the reception that would await him in England. With respect to the first of these, he seemed to have a particular dread of falling into the hands of the allies : the second was hopeless ; and the third, therefore, alone remained for him to adopt. Accordingly, on the 15th July, he was conveyed, in the French brig the *Epervier*, on board the Bellerophon, the Lieutenant of the former vessel receiving from Captain Maitland a written acknowledgment of the delivery of the person of Napoleon Buonaparte into his custody !

On the 16th the Bellerophon sailed for England. Buonaparte was accompanied by General Bertrand, Madame Bertrand, the Duke de Rovigo, General Lallemand, Baron Gourgaud, Count Montholon, the Countess his wife, Count Las Casas, and about fifty other individuals.

On the 24th July the Bellerophon arrived at Torbay, and the knowledge of the individual who was on board having reached England before, it became the general topic of conversation, while thousands went out to sea, in boats, yachts, &c. in the hope of obtaining a view of the captive. At first, he willingly gratified their curiosity, and appeared at the side of the ship, as if he was anxious to create a popular feeling in his favour : but when he found that it was determined he should not land in England, he became sullen, and seldom quitted his cabin.

While at Rochefort, he wrote the following letter to His Royal Highness the Prince Regent, which he no doubt imagined would inspire every exalted sentiment he could wish to find in the arbiters of his fate.

" ALTESSE ROYALE,

" En butte aux factions qui divisent mon pays, et à l'inimitié des plus grandes Puissances de l'Europe, j'ai terminé ma carriere politique ; et je viens, comme Thémistocle, m'asseoir sur les foyers du peuple Britannique. Je me mets sous la protection de ses lois, que je réclame de votre Altesse Royale comme le plus puissant, le plus constant, et le plus généreux, de mes ennemis.

" *Rochefort*, 13 *Juillet*, 1811.   " NAPOLEON."

This appeal preceded Napoleon's arrival on the English coast. It failed, however, to influence either the Regent or his Ministers; and it was determined that the island of St. Helena should be the place of his abode. When this was notified to him by Lord Keith, on the 3rd of August, he declared that he " would not go alive out of the Bellerophon;" that " he wished to establish himself in England;" that " England could only treat him as a prisoner of war," and that, if he went to St. Helena, " he should die in three months." He also wrote a formal protest against his removal, which he delivered to Lord Keith, the object of which was to shew that England would do herself immortal honor, by receiving him as her " guest;" and eternal infamy, by sending him to St. Helena.

On Sunday the 6th of August Lord Keith and Sir George Cockburn went on board the Bellerophon to inform Napoleon, that he, and such persons of his suite as would be permitted to accompany him, were to remove, on the following day, on board the Northumberland, which was appointed to convey him to St. Helena. Buonaparte again objected, most vehemently, to this decision on the part of the English government; but he at length named ten o'clock, as the hour when he would be ready to go on board the Northumberland. Accordingly, on Monday morning the 7th of August, he left the Bellerophon, and was received on board the Northumberland. When he arrived on deck, he took off his hat, and said to Sir G. Cockburn, " I am under your orders." He then bowed to Lord Lowther and Mr. Lyttleton, who were on board, and addressed a few words to them. He afterwards entered into a long conversation with them, and spoke freely upon many of the most remarkable political transactions of his life, such as the invasion of Spain and Russia, the Berlin and Milan decrees, &c.

On the 11th of August the Northumberland set sail for St. Helena, where it arrived on the 16th of October, after a long and tedious voyage. Buonaparte landed on the 18th. In that inglorious exile he may probably linger many years, a memorable example of the vicissitudes of human greatness. The most rigid precautions are adopted to prevent the possibility of his escape, and the wisdom of these precautions has been exemplified on more than one occasion since his abode in the island. Of those who accompanied him in his exile, three have since solicited and obtained permission to return to Europe. They are Las Casas, Montholon, and Gourgaud. They have all published accounts respecting Napoleon, but with so much of exaggeration and falshood, that very little reliance can be placed upon them.

DESCRIPTION OF THE MEDAL, No. XXXVII.

OBVERSE.—Bust of Buonaparte in his military uniform.

REVERSE.—A British man of war, in full sail, with the Imperial Eagle on the flag staff.

The Eagle on the staff is an admirable and satirical contrast to a Medal in the Napoleon series, by the Count Denon; in which Napoleon is represented as a Hercules at Boulogne, preparing for the invasion of England. Buonaparte is standing on the quarter deck. Another ship seen beyond. The legend — " SURRENDERED TO HIS BRITANNIC MAJESTY'S SHIP BELLEROPHON, CAPTAIN MAITLAND." On the exergue is the date of this event, " 15TH JULY, 1815." Brenet f. Mudie d.

DESCRIPTION OF No. XXXVIII.

OBVERSE.—Bust of Napoleon in his military uniform.

REVERSE.—Napoleon sitting pensively on the Island of St. Helena.
" Revolving in his altered mind
" The various turns of fate."

History is inciting him to record those annals of his life which Fame, as seen above, has already published. The Ships in the distance mark his situation as embosomed in the Sea, and as being imprisoned there by the maritime power of England.

This Medallic representation is a fine moral and satirical antithesis to the many boastful Medals of Napoleon, especially of that in which he has described England as a Monster, strangled by the power of France.

U

No. XXXIX.

ADMIRAL LORD EXMOUTH.

THIS gallant and distinguished officer entered very early into the naval service of his country, and during his long career has given many proofs of his skill and bravery. He was made a lieutenant in 1780, and soon after had an opportunity of distinguishing himself. In 1782, while commanding the Resolution cutter of 12 guns and 75 men in the channel, he fell in with the Flushing, a Dutch privateer of 24 guns and 68 men. A smart engagement followed, which continued for nearly two hours. In May, in the same year, he received his post captain's com-mission, and, at the close of the American war, he commanded La Nymphe frigate of 36 guns.

When the revolutionary war with France broke out, he had frequent opportunities of displaying his professional knowledge and intrepidity, nor did he ever let one of these opportunities escape. On the 18th of June 1793, being on a cruize, in company with the Venus frigate, Admiral Faulkner, he fell in with the French National frigate La Cleopatra, of 40 guns and 320 men, when, after a severe action which continued with singular fury for above half an hour, she surrendered to Captain Pellew. His gallantry did not go unrewarded. He had the honour of being introduced to his late Majesty by the Earl of Chatham, the first Lord of the Admiralty, and of receiving his Majesty's thanks, who also conferred upon him the rank of knighthood. In 1796 he was created a baronet of Great Britain ; and during the whole of that war, as well as the one which followed the rupture of the peace of Amiens, the name of Sir Edward Pellew constantly occurs in the naval exploits of the country. In 1814 his long services were rewarded by a peerage, to the dignity of which he was raised, on the 14th of May, by the title of Baron Exmouth of Cannonteign in the county of Devon.

His hour of repose, however, from the toils and perils of war, was not yet come. He was destined to twine one more wreath of laurel round the national banner, and to close a series of unexampled achievements by the navy of England, by one, nothing inferior to any of them. We allude to his gallant bombardment of Algiers, to commemorate the renown of which is the object of the present medal. This was a triumph peculiarly worthy of England, because it was obtained, not for the sake of ambition, nor for purposes of aggrandizement, but to advance the general interests of humanity.

His lordship set sail with a fleet, consisting of his own ship the Queen Charlotte, of 110 guns, the Impregnable of 98, three of 70 guns, the Leander of 50 guns, four more frigates, and several smaller armed vessels. Having rendezvoused at Gibraltar, and received there five gun-boats, he departed from that port on the 14th August 1816. He was joined, in the daring, but glorious enterprize by a Dutch squadron (commanded by Admiral Van Capellan) of five frigates and a sloop, which proved itself worthy of sharing with England the honour and the peril of the undertaking.

Before Lord Exmouth left Gibraltar he had received information which fully prepared him to expect a determined resistance. He was not disappointed. Considerable works were thrown up at Algiers, not only on both flanks of the city, but immediately above the entrance of the mole, and a large army was assembled for its defence. The combined fleets did not arrive before the bay of Algiers till the 27th of August, in consequence of calms and adverse winds. On that day Lord Exmouth dispatched a boat with a flag of truce, bearing the demands he was enjoined to make, on the part of the Prince Regent. They were, the immediate delivery of all christian slaves without ransom, the restitution of the money which had been already received for the Sardinian and Neapolitan captives, a solemn declaration from the Dey that he would, in future wars, treat prisoners according to the usage of European nations, and peace with the kingdom of the Netherlands on the like terms as those with the Prince Regent of England.

These demands were rejected, and his Lordship immediately prepared to enforce them. He had directed every preparation to be made for an attack, and now gave the signal to know if all the ships were ready.

Being answered in the affirmative, he bore up in the Queen Charlotte, followed by the fleet, for their appointed stations. The flag ship was anchored at the entrance of the mole, at the distance of about fifty yards. A profound silence prevailed, when a shot was fired at the Admiral's ship, which was then being lashed to the mainmast of an Algerine brig, close to the shore at the mouth of the mole ; and two more shots at the ships following.

Algiers, which contains a population of 80,000 souls, rises with an awful abruptness from the water's edge, to a great height. The batteries are one above another, strongly constructed and fortified. Sweeping from the western extremity is a tongue of land, which defends the entrance to the inner part of the harbour, and also the approach to it. Along the whole of this tongue was a range of strong batteries, which ships must pass to take their station near the town, in order to bombard it.

The position of the Queen Charlotte was at the extreme point of the tongue above described, by which she enfiladed the whole line of batteries along it. She was so near that every part of the mole, and what is called the Marine, was visible from the quarter deck. Both these places were crowded with spectators, who seemed as if they expected no firing. Lord Exmouth, with a humanity which did him honour, ascended the poop of his vessel, and waved his hat, as a warning for these people to retire : but the signal was not attended to, and the first broadside swept off some hundreds of them. The other ships took their stations with admirable coolness and precision : and a fire more tremendous than was, perhaps, ever before witnessed, immediately commenced on both sides. It was maintained from a quarter before three, until nine, without intermission, and continued, partially, for two hours longer. The flotilla of mortar, gun, and rocket-boats, was ably conducted, and it was by its fire that all the ships in the port, with the exception of one frigate, were involved in flames. The conflagration spread rapidly over the whole arsenal, store-house, and gun boats, affording a spectacle of awful grandeur beyond the power of description. The enemies' batteries around the Admiral's division were silenced about ten o'clock, and reduced to a state of perfect ruin, but it was not until two in the morning that the fleet could be towed off out of reach of those forts whose fire was still kept up.

Although the close of the combat was such as to indicate the probability of its being renewed on the following day, its events were so decisive that Lord Exmouth felt himself justified in assuming the tone of a conqueror. . Accordingly next morning, he despatched a letter to the Dey, offering the same terms of peace as before, but with the proviso that neither the British Consul, nor the detained naval officers and men, should have been treated with cruelty, and that they should be sent off to the fleet. If these conditions were not acceded to, the bombardment would be re-commenced at the convenience of his Lordship. After a consideration of three hours, however, the Dey thought it more prudent to comply, and a conference was held on board the flag ship, which ended in the signature of a treaty of peace. The principal conditions of this treaty were, the abolition for ever, of christian slavery; and the delivery to Lord Exmouth of all slaves in the dominions of the Dey, to whatever nation they might belong. There were other stipulations, some of them personally humiliating to the Dey, and some intended to guard against the repetition of those tyrannous practices which had provoked this merited chastisement. When the combined fleets sailed from Algiers on the 3rd of September, the British Admiral was gratified with the heart-felt triumph of knowing that he had not left a single christian prisoner behind him.

Upon his return to England the noble Lord was further advanced to the dignity of Viscount Exmouth, September 21, 1816.

DESCRIPTION OF THE MEDAL.

OBVERSE.—Bust of Lord Exmouth.

REVERSE.—The superiority and grandeur of Britain on the Ocean, are here typified by Neptune controuling a Sea-Horse, which, from the inscription on the exergue—" ALGIERS, AUGUST, 1816," more immediately relates to the successful attack on the chief piratical state of Barbary.

No. XL.

THE IONIAN ISLANDS.

THE sovereignty of these islands was secured to the crown of Great Britain by a treaty with the Emperor of Russia, which was signed at Paris on the 5th of November 1815. The first article of this treaty declares that the islands of Corfu, Cephalonia, Zante, Santa, Maura, Ithaca, Cerigo, and Paxo, with their dependencies, shall form a single, free, and independent state, under the denomination of the United States of the Ionian Islands. The second article provides, that this state shall be placed under the immediate and exclusive protection of His Majesty the King of Great Britain, his heirs and successors. The remaining articles, which are six in number, stipulate the general conditions upon which this transfer of sovereignty is made, such as the appointment of a Lord High Commissioner, the convocation of a legislative assembly to draw up a constitutional charter, the recognition of the flag of the United States of the Ionian Islands as the flag of a free and independent state, &c.

In pursuance of the 4th article of the Treaty, a "Constitutional Chart of the United States of the Ionian Islands" was unanimously agreed upon, and passed by the Legislative Assembly on the 2nd of May 1817. This chart consists of seven chapters relating, 1. to the general organization of the Ionian Islands ; 2. the Senate ; 3. the Legislative Assembly ; 4. Local Governments ; 5. Ecclesiastical Establishments ; 6. the Judicial Authority ; and 7. certain miscellaneous regulations, such as the army, finance, foreign relations, &c. &c. It would be quite foreign from the purpose of this work, to analyse this charter ; but we may glance at two or three points of general import. The seat of the government is declared to be permanently fixed in the capital of the island of Corfu. The established religion is the orthodox greek religion, but all other forms of the christian religion are protected. The general language of the states is declared to be Greek. The civil government of the states is composed of a Legislative Assembly, of a Senate, and of a Judicial authority. The legislative assembly is elected from the body " of the noble electors." The senators are elected out of the body of the legislative assembly. The judicial body is elected by the senate : and these elections and all other civil appointments are declared valid for five years, except under certain specified circumstances. The power of assembling and proroguing Parliament is vested in the Lord High Commissioner; but the power of dissolving it is solely vested in his Majesty by an order in Council. The Parliament cannot be prorogued for a longer space than six months. Upon the whole, this constitution may be regarded as well adapted to secure the freedom and prosperity of the Ionian Islands, and we doubt not the inhabitants already find reason to rejoice that they are under the mild sway of the British sceptre. This, indeed, is sufficiently proved, in the latest official document which has been received from these states. We allude to the address of the Lord High Commissioner, on the 7th March 1820, to the Legislative Assembly, in which His Excellency dwells with great emphasis, upon the advantages already derived, and those that are likely to ensue from the constitution of 1817.

DESCRIPTION OF THE MEDAL.

OBVERSE.—Britannia with Tables of the Laws she is about to give to the Ionian Islands. Neptune is introduced as emblematical of the naval power by which the means were afforded of conferring those Laws.

REVERSE.—Seven Females, the number of the Ionian Islands, exultingly moving round their protecting British Flag.

FINIS.

www.ingramcontent.com/pod-product-compliance
Lightning Source LLC
Chambersburg PA
CBHW081552110426
42743CB00047BA/3128